# Chasing the ~~Sun~~ Son

*the*

**A lyrically inspired devotional for
Christ's searching, wandering,
questioning followers**

BRITTANY WILHELM

WestBow Press books may be ordered through booksellers or by contacting:

WestBow Press
A Division of Thomas Nelson & Zondervan
1663 Liberty Drive
Bloomington, IN 47403
www.westbowpress.com
844-714-3454

Scripture quotations marked CSB have been taken from the Christian Standard Bible®, Copyright © 2017 by Holman Bible Publishers. Used by permission. Christian Standard Bible® and CSB® are federally registered trademarks of Holman Bible Publishers.

all photography is the author's own

ISBN: 978-1-6642-1968-7 (sc)
ISBN: 978-1-6642-1969-4 (e)

Library of Congress Control Number: 2021901545

Print information available on the last page.

WestBow Press rev. date: 02/17/2021

WESTBOW
P R E S S®
A DIVISION OF THOMAS NELSON
& ZONDERVAN

Dedicated to Christopher, for tirelessly supporting, encouraging, and inspiring me, but mostly, for loving me completely. To Alex, for helping me remember that, with God's help, we can do hard things; and to Dad, for raising me to question everything and always seek to understand the truth.

With special, heartfelt gratitude to Pastors Wayne Darbonne, Jim Stuart, and Craig Thighe for their generous guidance, wisdom, and unwavering support.

# Contents

# Introduction

My soul was stirring. I was anxious and anticipating, nervous and curious, uncertain and searching. God was inviting me to trust him. To ask. To listen. To obey. And I tried…but how do you listen for God? I looked for direction in his word (John 1:1), I listened for his still, small voice (1 Kings 19:11-13), and I watched for his signs and deeds (Psalm 92:4-5). But when I searched the Bible, I was overwhelmed, not knowing where to start. When I tried to listen, I heard nothing but silence. When I tried to be alert for signs, I missed them. I know that God is ever present, everywhere, every moment…so how can he be so hard to find? Not knowing what else to do, I did the one thing that 15 years of non-profit administration has taught me to do: I called a meeting.

Yes, I called a meeting with God. I know that sounds either brazen or foolish, but nonetheless, I set a time and a place, I committed to being there, and I asked (or begged) God to join me. It went something like this: "Lord, I know that you are everywhere, but right now, my finite mind is having a hard time really grasping you in your infinite being and omnipresence. I really need to talk to you, and much more importantly, I need to hear you and listen to you. Starting tomorrow, I will wait at the park each morning at sunrise. Will you come?" And he did.

The first morning I walked to our small neighborhood park, I was enveloped in silence. Windows were beginning to light up, but the road was perfectly quiet, perfectly still, and it was just me and God. When I arrived, I sat on a bench facing east, and settled in for a front-row view of the sun pouring out over God's creation. As I watched, calmly and expectantly, the darkness faded in a beautiful splash of color. I asked God to let me know if he was there, and at that exact moment, the song in my headphones (So Will I by Hillsong Worship) celebrated the rising sun and praised the artwork of God's creation. It was as if my shuffled playlist knew I was looking out at the painted sky and searching for his presence.

I kept my appointment each morning, day after day, and I waited. I trusted God to use this time to reveal his will for me, to strengthen me, to renew me, to guide me, to nudge (or shove) me, and to restore me (Isaiah 40:31). I listened for more lyrical messages in the soundtrack of each walk, and I took time to learn more when I didn't understand. As I faithfully gave the first part of my day to the Lord, I found myself in awe of what he did with the rest of it. The more I listened, the deeper I explored, and the more I learned. Then it happened, suddenly and inexplicably, scripture began to resonate in new ways, small pulls on my heart began to feel audible, and people crossed my path in new and unnerving ways. Although God, in his grace and love, "met me" at my request, when I turned myself over to him, when I stopped expecting God to reveal himself on my terms, I started to find him on his.

As you read, explore, listen, and pray through these pages, I hope that my journey might help you on yours. I pray that God will reveal himself to us both, in his perfect timing. And through our respective journeys, I pray that we will learn to trust him more fully, to follow him more faithfully, to serve him more obediently, and to love him more completely.

*I believe in Christianity as I believe that the sun has risen,*
*not only because I see it, but because by it, I see everything else.*

*– C.S. Lewis*

# *Day One: Intention*

🎧 *Suggested Streaming: So Will I (1 Billion X) by Hillsong Worship*

With my *Contemporary Christian* playlist set to shuffle, I was ready to go! At the top of the hill, I turned to see the sun just beginning to crest over the horizon, and in that exact moment, Hillsong Worship streamed through my headphones praising, what else? The rising sun. I laughed a little to myself, thinking that sometimes God subtly tells us whether we're on the right track…but other times, he literally sings it to your soul. Thank you, Lord, for this clear affirmation.

With this sign, I made a mental note to continue listening each day with an open heart, and to thoughtfully consider what God may choose to convey in the soundtrack of this new daily journey. I am reminded that Paul urged the Ephesians to "…be filled with the Spirit, speaking to one another with psalms, hymns, and songs from the Spirit. Sing and make music from your heart to the Lord (Ephesians 5:18-19)." With due respect to the Apostle Paul, I will leave the actual singing to Hillsong (trust me, it's better that way), but I am encouraged by this reminder that God will use even the most unexpected channels, and all we have to do is listen and be still.

For today, the first day of this devotional, our purpose is simple: walk with gratitude and begin building a more intentional discipline of prayer. As I look down at my Bible, I am stilled by the familiar verse embroidered on its cover: "Rejoice always, pray without ceasing, and in everything give thanks (1 Thessalonians 5:16-18)," which is a clear, direct instruction from Paul's letter to the church in Thessalonica. In this guidance, Paul reminds us that prayer was never intended to be a morning, bedtime, or pre-meal ritual, but rather, that it is a powerful channel each of us has directly to our Creator and our Savior. If we cultivate a habit of prayer – always, without ceasing, in everything – then we open a dialog with God that weaves intricately through every aspect of our lives. By rejoicing, we glorify him and testify his goodness and the grace he extends (and that we do not deserve). By praying, we ask for his intercession and acknowledge his sovereign, limitless power. And by giving thanks for everything, we humble ourselves and foster gratitude for all that God has done and is doing in our lives.

What an incredible opportunity God has extended to us, this wide-open, always accessible, always active channel of communication. God is listening. To you, to me, to all of us. No matter how big our request, great our concern, complex our challenge, or worrisome our fear, God is listening intently, and he cares deeply. He tells us, "pray to me, and I will listen to you. You will seek me and find me when you search for me with all your heart...Call to me and I will answer you and tell you great and incomprehensible things you do not know (Jeremiah 29: 12-12, 33:3)." David knew this to be true, and he wrote in Psalm 18:6, "I called to the Lord in my distress and I cried to my God for help. From his temple he heard my voice, and my cry to him reached his ears." We can learn so much from this posture as we strive to cultivate a habit of prayer that is not a ritual practice, but rather, something as natural, essential, and automatic as our hearts beating, lungs breathing, and eyes opening.

### A Prayer

*Thank you, Lord, for always listening. Thank you for opening the channel of prayer that we may approach you constantly, no matter the purpose or circumstance. Help me to remember that prayer is neither confined to specific times or routines during my day, nor is it a one-way channel. Thank you for inviting us to commune and converse with you in this way, and please help me to accept that invitation, as Paul suggested, unceasingly. Amen.*

# Day Two: Direction

🎧 *Suggested Streaming: Hills and Valleys by Tauren Wells*

Today I felt like I truly was *chasing* the sun. After leaving a few minutes late and fearing I would miss the sunrise, I ran rather than walked, and arrived (breathless and embarrassingly out of shape) with this beautiful song reminding me that we are always standing in the love of God, no matter where we may find ourselves. I realized I don't have to run to catch God, and I can never "just miss" him. He is wherever I am. Yet, the question of "where?" pulls on our hearts all the time, doesn't it? Where we are, where we aren't, where we ought to be, where we have left behind. We wonder where our careers might lead, where our families will journey to, and where we will be led. When we've decided where we're going, how will we know if we're called there by grace, by opportunity, by ambition, by desire, or by faith?

"Where?" is the question that started me on this journey – I know I am seeking guidance, grace, wisdom, and direction…but where? No matter how lost we feel at times, we have to remember that none of us is – nor can we ever be – anywhere or in any place that God didn't intentionally and lovingly place us. It's frustrating when we feel restless, unhappy, or ready for a change, but timing is everything, even when patience is hard to muster. Peter reminds, "don't forget this one thing, dear friends: with the Lord a day is like a thousand years, and a thousand years are like a day. The Lord is not slow in keeping his promise, as some understand slowness. He is patient with you, not wanting anyone to perish…" (2 Peter 3:8-9).

In a world and a culture that thrives on instant gratification, how do we cultivate patience? Not just any patience, but the kind of patience that empowers us to wait through times we want to escape from, for as long as it takes for God to prepare us for whatever may come next. The kind of patience that is so deeply rooted in trust that we know, with unwavering confidence, that He is working all things for our good (Romans 8:28). As we wait, we pray for patience and peace in our restlessness, try to be still, try to listen, and try to obey, always remembering that no matter where we are, his love surrounds us.

### *A Prayer*

*Father I thank you for your perfect timing and your plans for me, which I know are plans for my good. Please help me to be patient in the waiting and help me to look for the ways in which you are using this period to prepare me for what comes next. Comfort me and help me not to try and rush ahead to the next step, but help me to be prepared and willing when the moment comes. Father, remind me that I can't miss you, nor can I miss out on all you have planned for me, as long as I keep my heart and eyes fixed on you. Amen.*

# Day Three: Rest in Suffering

🎧 *Suggested Streaming: Go Rest High on That Mountain by Vince Gill*

Rather than walking to the park near my house, this morning I woke up in beautiful Beaver Creek, Colorado. Beaver Creek is one of the most breathtaking places in all of creation, especially this time of year, with the aspens turning from green to spectacular yellows and oranges, the mountain air crisp and fresh, and the kind of peaceful silence that allows you to find comfort in a giant, complex world. Even without the structure of my new morning routine, I try to be alert – ready to hear and listen to whatever God may be trying to tell me today, ready to rise to whatever occasion he calls me to, ready for anything – but all I hear is, well, nothing. Deafening silence.

After a long silence in the beautiful Rocky Mountains, a song came to mind from deep in my heart with the force of a freight train. It wasn't Chris Tomlin, Lauren Daigle, or Mercy Me, but clear as day, Vince Gill's voice rang in my ears. It's a song that has dual meanings for me – first, and perhaps most obviously, "rest." The call to look around and embrace the time, the moment, the beauty, and to rest while we are surrounded by the glory of God's creation (especially when it is lit ablaze in a firestorm of autumn colors!). It is almost as if God's voice is urging us - rest while you are within the beauty of my canvas. Rest, even while there is work to be done. Rest, and know that I am in control, I am here with you, and I am not letting go. Rest, and know that I am (Exodus 3:14).

Even as I attempt to slow my racing mind and live into this peaceful moment, memories of this song also flood my heart with pain that's more powerful than that peace. Thinking of the beautiful melody recalls the sound of its graceful lyrics playing over stifled cries at my mom's funeral. The song, which describes the end of a life that was riddled with trouble and pain, captured her struggle so perfectly and so poetically. Hearing it in the corners of my mind, in turn, brings back feelings of guilt, anger, wariness, distrust, and regret over forgiveness that I afforded too late.

It's hard to hold such powerful, competing emotions in our minds at the same time. Rest, but face your sorrow. Rest, but live into your pain. Rest, but honor your shortcomings. Rest, but mourn your losses. How are we to rest while also living these real, human experiences? And then the answer comes:

*Rest. Be still and know that I am God. (Psalm 46:10).*

It's unnerving the way God works within the most tragic moments of our lives, offering comfort that humans simply aren't able to provide . A well-meaning friend may offer platitudes like, "this too shall pass" or "it's always darkest before the dawn", but no one ever says that when it's their storm that isn't passing or their night that isn't breaking. Instead, in those moments, we ask, "why?" One word. One question. One demand. We beg, plead, and pray to know why. We question why our God, a good, loving, infinitely powerful God, would allow this to happen. Even Jesus asked, as he cried out from the cross in anguish, "Eloi, Eloi, lama sabachthani?" – My God, my God, why have you forsaken me? (Matthew 27:46). It is in those moments, in the moments when everything is crumbling, including and especially our hearts, the Lord says to us, Rest. Be still. I am here. I am with you. I am able to use this for your good, in ways that go far beyond anything you can imagine (Ephesians 3:20). I can and I will be with you, because *I am*.

This simple, yet profoundly important truth is the cornerstone of where we can find real rest, comfort, and peace. To know that God is our refuge and strength, even if the earth gives way and the mountains fall into the ocean (Psalm 46:1-3). Even then, we can feel the presence of the one who has gone ahead of us, and who will never leave nor forsake us (Deuteronomy 31:8). Sometimes our world gets shaken, and we don't understand, and won't pretend that it's okay. We try to hide our pain and our broken hearts. But we trust, and we search for the unexpected glimpses of beauty that surface from the depths of pain. In doing so, we can rejoice in the suffering, for we know and embrace that it fosters perseverance, and perseverance character, and character hope (Romans 5:3).

### A Prayer

*Thank you, Lord, for always being with me, and for helping me to know that I can rest even while the storms rage on, because you are here. When I am facing loss or heartbreak, please hold on tighter and remind me that you will not forsake me. When the storms do pass, help me to remember that you saw me through, and help me to see how persevering through them has brought me to the hope and beauty on the other side. Amen.*

# Day Four: Clinging to the Vine

🎧 *Suggested Streaming: Best News Ever by MercyMe*

I try to protect this time each morning, blocking out thoughts and focusing my heart and my mind on communion with God, but sometimes I can't stop the tidal wave of stressful thoughts from breaking through – family, work, friends, church, chores, and a dozen other obligations and opportunities. As I approach the top of the hill still trying to calm my mind, this song urged me, not to forget my worries and burdens, but simply to put them in better perspective.

Without disregarding or devaluing the truly countless blessings in my life, I confess that I find myself running on empty most days – constantly pushing my productivity with more plans and new tools, pushing my energy with more caffeine and new vitamins, and pushing myself to be more available to everyone for everything. Whenever I start to feel this way (which is basically my normal state of being) I fall back on John 15 – The Vine and the Branches. In this poetically crafted metaphor, Jesus reminds us that we are like branches fixed to a vine. As long as we cling to the vine, it will nourish, support, and sustain us. Through the branches (us), the vine will bear fruit. Branches wither on their own, they cannot bear fruit themselves, but as long as the branch abides in the vine, and the vine in the branch, the fruit will come. It's important that we remember this each time we search for success on our own terms or allow competing demands and expectations to overwhelm our hearts. As we work and toil away, often to indeterminant ends, we have to pause and remember that our charge is not to bear fruit. Our charge is not to try the hardest, work the longest, nor push the farthest to produce good works. Our charge, purely and simply, is to cling to the vine, and in so doing, allow the vine to create, nurture, grow, and harvest fruit through us.

This imagery centers us in what – or rather who – our focus ought to be on, but let's also consider how vineyard branches meet and entangle themselves with other branches. A branch's path is never solitary, it seeks support and direction, companionship in a way, from other branches. Nor is my path a solitary one. I have benefitted greatly from other "branches" I have encountered, and I have also been threatened and challenged by some. Some I have intertwined my life with and others I have grown away from, but all have shaped and influenced my path. From the very beginning, God knew the importance of companionship for those whom He created in his image. In Genesis, God says, "it is not good for the man to be alone. I will make a helper suitable for him." (Genesis 2:18), and the Book of Proverbs is also filled with encouragement to engage others in our lives and our walks, while exercising caution and being selective of the company we keep: "Whoever walks with the wise becomes wise, but a companion of fools suffers harm." (Proverbs 13:20); "As iron sharpens iron, so one man sharpens another." (Proverbs 27:17); and "Do not make friends with a hot-tempered man, do not associate with one easily angered, or you may learn his ways and get yourself ensnared." (Proverbs 22:24-25).

Beyond clinging to Jesus and engaging with others, Jesus' metaphor also offers guidance that most of us would rather do without…acknowledging that healthy, thriving branches require a lot of pruning. "He cuts off every branch in me that bears no fruit, while every branch that does bear fruit he prunes, so that it will be even more fruitful (John 15:2)". Careful, constant tending may feel painful and destructive at first, but it is necessary for the branch to thrive. We have all been cut before, sometimes just a small trim and sometimes deeply – to the core. We have been burned. We have been pulled (yanked!) in directions we would not have chosen ourselves. Every one of those experiences refines us in some way, makes us stronger, reminds us of our true charge – clinging to the vine – and better prepares us to bear fruit in a stressful life and a broken world. Max Lucado articulates this beautifully in *Anxious for Nothing*, "Our assignment is not fruitfulness, but faithfulness" because "the dominant duty of the branch is to cling to the vine."

### *A Prayer*

*Lord, thank you for working in me and through me, as long as I abide in you. Thank you for pruning me, even when it hurts, and for giving me strength, knowing that you will work through me to produce whatever fruit – whatever good works – you require. Please grant me discernment as I encounter and engage with other "branches" in your Kingdom, and help me to build relationships with those who strengthen my connection to you. Lord, today and for all of my days, help me cling to the vine. Amen.*

# Day Five: It is Well

🎧 *Suggested Streaming: Even If by MercyMe*

After just five days on this journey of curiosity, exploration, questioning, reflecting, remembering, and trusting, I feel a strong, powerful call to keep going; but, when I arrived at the park this morning I found my favorite bench already occupied. So I continued on as, once again, Mercy Me streamed into my headphones. This song quotes one of the most timeless and poetic hymns of all time, *It Is Well With My Soul*. The words settled deep into my heart, into my bones, and I knew my destination. Just a few blocks away is a memorial garden nestled behind the church we call home. The garden is beautiful; perfectly still and quiet. A path winds through trees and flowers toward a few humble stone benches and a cross – a tangible reminder of God's presence in this hallowed place, and a beautiful celebration of the eternal lives of those laid to rest in its soil. There is every reason to find peace in this outdoor sanctuary, except that in the middle of this wondrously beautiful garden rests the ashes of a baby boy. A 5 ½ month old child who loved, and laughed, and smiled, and babbled. It has been fourteen years since I held my son in my arms. I don't come to this place for peace nor for solitude. Until this morning, I have only ever come here for companionship – to feel close to him, to leave flowers in remembrance, to wish him happy birthday or Merry Christmas – my visits are always with a purpose, and usually with a heavy heart. With precious little resolve walking into the garden, I am echoing MercyMe's plea for strength.

The lyricist behind the well-known hymn *It Is Well With My Soul* has a story as inspiring as the song itself. After losing his two-year old son, becoming financially ruined by the Great Chicago Fire, and losing all four of his daughters in a shipwreck on the Atlantic Ocean, Horatio Spafford penned the lyrics aboard a ship as it passed over his children's watery grave. It was there, in the place that marked his deepest, greatest pain, that he wrote, "When sorrows like sea billows roll, whatever my lot, thou has taught me to say 'it is well, it is well with my soul.'" To experience that kind of faith, that kind of peace, even when your heart is broken and when you have no idea how to put it back together, to be washed – flooded – by a love that cannot be explained, understood, or even fathomed. The song is a sobering reminder that the condition of our souls is not dependent upon the condition of our bodies or even the sadness of our hearts or worries of our minds.

Paul urged the Philippians not to be anxious about anything, but to present their needs to God, and in doing so, "the peace of God, which transcends all understanding, will guard your hearts and your minds in Christ Jesus" (Philippians 4:6-7). Peace which transcends all understanding is just a prayer away – perfect, unexplainable, indescribable, absolute peace. It sounds too easy, doesn't it? If all it takes is whispering a prayer to feel the kind of soul-embracing peace Horatio Spafford sang of, why are so many of us living without it? It seems that finding peace is something quite different from embracing it, surrendering to it, and living it.

I often wonder if we hold back from asking for peace because we aren't ready to have it. Maybe we're clinging to some sense of justification that comes from dwelling in our pain a little longer, or perhaps we think we don't deserve it, that accepting peace is in some way a betrayal of whatever it is we're grieving. What we have to remember is that Christ died to give us access to the Father's transcendent peace. Even when our bodies or our hearts are broken, it is well with our souls.

### A Prayer

*Heavenly Father, thank you for your indescribable peace. In the broken world we live in, in the chaos that surrounds us, and in the very real and painful battles we face, it seems impossible that peace can or should be found. Yet you offer it to us in abundance if we are only willing to accept it. Help me today to see past the fears I face and, entrusting them fully to you, to join the hymn writer in rejoicing that "it is well, it is well with my soul". Amen.*

# Day Six: Faith

🎧 *Suggested Streaming: Oceans (Where Feet May Fall) by Hillsong UNITED*

This morning the sun seemed hidden and did not rush to greet me as it has all week. Instead, clouds settled in across the sky, along with an icy chill and a hushed, somewhat ominous darkness. As the changing seasons enveloped me, the words of one of my favorite songs did too. This song is a beautiful tribute to the moment when Jesus is seen walking on water, and Peter calls out to him, "Lord, if it is you, tell me to come to you on the water." So Jesus replies, "Come." (Matthew 14: 28-29). It is a moment is so moving because on some level, I think we all strive to have faith like that. Faith that tells us even when we are scared and even in moments of doubt, we can still step out with confidence into the deepest waters, amidst the darkest storm.

While it takes pretty remarkable faith to trust that Jesus will give you the ability to walk, one foot in front of the other, on top of the sea, I especially admire Peter for what came before that leap (or step) of faith. When Jesus assured the terrified disciples, "Take courage, it is I. Don't be afraid." as He walked toward them on the open, stormy waters (Matthew 14:27), Paul did something extraordinary. He asked Jesus to reveal himself, and through him, to reveal his greatness. He beckoned to Jesus, "If it's really you, then tell me to come to you. (Matthew 14:28)" I am confident that Peter knew it was Jesus (assuming there wasn't a lot of foot traffic on the open waves), which means he also knew that Christ would respond affirmatively and tell him to come. Jesus would use that moment and Peter's faithful obedience to work in ways that Peter could barely fathom.

Although Peter's faith still faltered when he allowed his heart to focus on the waves instead of the Lord, I give Peter a lot of credit for even asking. How often do we stop short of asking God to reveal his true power, even (or perhaps especially) when we know what He will say? Peter knew that Christ, the Son of Man, would certainly tell him to step out onto the crashing waves, and when He did, Peter knew he would have to take that step. Perhaps Peter's real act of faith was not in stepping out onto the ocean, but in asking the Lord to bid him to. I know there have been times, probably more than I can count, when I have allowed fear to intervene and I have fallen short of

Peter's example. Afraid my feet would fail, that the waves would overtake me, afraid of unknown dangers lurking beneath the surface, or worse, afraid that I would have to follow whatever scary path the Lord sets me out on, I have stopped short not only of following God's direction, but sometimes of even asking for it. Uncertain of how the Lord will intercede, but certain that I am not prepared for any intercession that doesn't fit into my carefully thought-out plan, I hesitate to even ask Jesus to reveal his true power and nature in my life.

The Hillsong UNITED song ends by repeating a beautiful refrain – a plea, a prayer, a courageous request – that God would lead us to a place beyond our comfort zone. A place where all we can do is trust him, and that we would go willingly by the strength of our faith alone. What an incredible act of faith, to say to the God who created the universe, "Whatever you want me to do, I will do. I trust your plan and I will obey your will in my life." The cry to be led, even when we don't know where we are being led to, is a statement of pure unabashed faith. It is the kind of faith Isaiah had when he answered the Lord's call bravely, "Here I am. Send me." (Isaiah 6:8) – but where to? The verses that follow this inspiring statement contain an impossible charge. God bids Isaiah to carry a message that He knows the people will not listen to, share news they will refuse to hear, and to continue doing so until the land and all of its cities are destroyed, and all the people sent out. (Isaiah 6:9-12). But what comes after this impossible message? Hope. Enduring and unequivocal hope. In verse 13, God goes on to tell Isaiah, "But as the terebinth and oak leave stumps when they are cut down, so the holy seed will be the stump in the land." It is a powerful reminder that God does not call us to carry out his will in our way, nor is his role to sanction and rubber-stamp our plans – even if they are plans that we intend for his service. Isaiah's obedience was more important to God than his success or achievement, because God had a much larger plan than Isaiah could have possibly understood, and he had a very specific role to play in it.

### A Prayer

*Lord, thank you for using us to carry out your divine will and plans. Like Peter, I pray that you would grant me faith to step out onto the waters, confident that you will guide, protect, and lead me, even when my circumstances feel stormy and unsafe. Please help me learn to put obedience ahead of ambition, so that as I am called to play my part in your great plan, like Isaiah, I will respond, "Here I am. Send me." Not for my will, not for my purposes, not for my desires, but for yours. Amen.*

# Day Seven: Pathways

🎧 *Suggested Streaming: God Help Me by Plumb*

Okay. Here I am, Lord! Where will you send me? What is the next step in this journey? Where does this path lead? What is your will?

I am a planner – possibly to a fault. I like to be aware, prepared, and ready to change course when needed. I very rarely do anything without an end game in mind, and my contingency plans have contingency plans. Perhaps that is what makes this moment, this season, feel so difficult. Lord, I have no idea where you would have me go. I feel an intense, unsettling sense of change and a shifting in my soul, but without your direction, it feels a little panicked and somewhat frenetic. As I approached the sunrise today, and as I approached the Lord and his alter, these feelings of restlessness were pulling hard at my heart as Plumb's song cried out to God, begging him to show me the way forward.

The word "path" appears over 100 times in the Bible, as do references to walking alongside God and walking with one another. The idea that we desire, and are called, to move forward along a path the Lord has cultivated for us is compelling, and it calls to mind familiar imagery from the 23rd Psalm, "He leads me beside still waters. He restores my soul. He leads me along paths of righteousness for his name's sake (Psalm 23:2-3)". The verse continues, "even though I walk through the valley of the shadow of death, I will fear no evil, for you are with me." The prophet Isaiah also touches on paths of righteousness, assuring the people of Israel that "the path of the righteous is level; O upright one, you make the way of the righteous smooth (Isaiah 26:7)." This sentiment of living and walking with God along the path he curates and makes straight for us is echoed in both the Psalms and the Proverbs: "All the paths of the Lord are loving and faithful for those who keep the demands of his covenant (Psalm 25:10) and even more directly, "Trust in the Lord with all your heart and lean not on your won understanding; in all your ways acknowledge him and he will make your paths straight (Proverbs 3:5-6)."

It is striking how clearly we are told that when we live in ways that honor God's teachings, our paths will be straight, they will progress upon level terrain, and proceed by still waters – but it often doesn't feel that way. Our paths feel stuttered and winding, uphill and down, along still waters and stormy seas; yet when the path feels scary, there is comfort in knowing we are never alone, and every step is illuminated for us. We are never alone, because God actively draws nearer as we humble ourselves to submit to his will, his plan, the path he has mapped. James tells us, "Come near to God and he will come near to you…Humble yourselves before the Lord and he will lift you up (James 4:8, 10)," and the prophet Micah urged that what the Lord requires of us is "To seek justice, love mercy, and walk humbly with your God (Micah 6:8)." When we walk with God, when we seek his companionship and direction (and forgo our own), God draws near to us. He walks with us, and if God is with us, who could possibly be against us? (Romans 8:31).

In keeping with this pathway metaphor for our lives, God not only charted the path and traverses it with us, he also intentionally lights our way forward. Psalm 119 says, "I gain understanding from your precepts; therefore, I hate every wrong path. Your work is a lamp to my feet and a light for my path (Psalm 119: 104-105)". Picture this "lamp to your feet". It is not a hand-held lantern, a streetlamp, or even a headlamp, but specifically, *a lamp to our feet*. A lamp to our feet would, presumably, illuminate only the immediate next step – and how often does God chose to do exactly that in our lives? He knows we would be overwhelmed, intimidated, scared, or reluctant if we saw the entire road ahead with all its risks and uncertainties, twists and turns, valleys and peaks. Yet, he knows it is a path that leads to our good and to the good of his Kingdom, so he shows us and guides us – one step at a time.

How often do we plead with God to tell us his will for our lives? How often do we ask him to just give us the map and let us lead the way? But how much better, how much more wonderful will it be if we simply place our faith and trust in the one who not only drew the map, but who created the very terrain upon which we tread?

### *A Prayer*

*Lord, please help my willful heart to trust and surrender fully to you. Please help me to humble myself to forget all I think I know about my future, so that I may faithfully, confidently, and courageously place one foot in front of the other on this path you've created, though I may not know where it leads. Father, I know very often the best path is the longest way around, and I ask you to give me the strength and faith to carry forward. Amen.*

# Day Eight: Fear and Fellowship

🎧 *Suggested Streaming: Need You Now by Plumb*

This morning as I walked, I caught myself constantly looking over my shoulder. The walk is dark, and even though my path weaves through a safe neighborhood that I know well, I couldn't shake the (completely unwarranted) sense of imminent danger. As I walked with the weight of this feeling, it occurred to me how often we find ourselves living in the midst of fear. Whether personally or on a more universal scale, fear is the driving force behind a great many of our decisions and actions. As I listened to Plumb's song this morning, which cries out with fear and a need for God to stay close, I am stricken by how completely undone we are when we're afraid. Fear, more than almost any other emotion, has the power to truly overwhelm – to paralyze us or make us frenetic, to focus us or scramble our minds, to inspire us or break us.

Knowing the iron grip fear has over our hearts, minds, and actions, God constantly seeks to reassure us of his presence. In fact, God's guidance to "fear not" or "do not be afraid" appears in the Bible over 100 times, including a personal favorite verse, "Fear not, for I am with you; do not be afraid for I am your God. I will strengthen you; I will help you; I will hold onto you with my righteous right hand. (Isaiah 41:10)." Fear is so much more daunting and more debilitating when we feel as though we are facing it alone – but as we know, God is with us always, and if God is for us, who (or what) can be against us? (Romans 8:31). Whether we are facing unexpected loss, navigating uncertain terrain, living through global crises, or the myriad of fears along and beyond that spectrum, our comfort in times of fear can often be found in fellowship. People are made for community, for friendship, for partnership.

From the very beginning, the Lord knew, "It is not good for the man to be alone (Genesis 2:18)." Alone, we imagine the worst, we convince ourselves that the world and our circumstances within it are too great, too daunting, too overwhelming to overcome. Yet solidarity, empathy, shared understanding, and mutual experiences ease our fears exponentially. When we are "in it together", whatever we face feels bearable, manageable, even conquerable.

I don't think it is coincidence that the Bible references loving one another – our neighbors – as ourselves, almost as many times as it tells us not to be afraid. Jesus told the Pharisees that the commandment to love your neighbor is the second most important commandment, preceded only by the command to love your God with all your heart, soul, and mind. He even asserted that the entirety of the law and prophets hang on those two commandments (Matthew 22:37-40). Not only does loving each other foster the community and fellowship that abates fear, but it also reminds and inspires us to look beyond ourselves and our own circumstances. When we love one another, we act with greater grace, mercy, humility, compassion, and perspective, and those extend well beyond our fears.

The true and fundamental power of fear, whether uniquely personal or shared worldwide, is rooted in isolation. The loneliness that grips our hearts when we think the walls are caving in as the sky falls to pieces around us, is crippling. Walking alone in the shadows, as the song describes, is terrifying, but when someone walks beside us and stays with us each step along the way, the fear becomes shared, the burden lifted communally, and the weight of it all becomes manageable. In loving each other, reaching out to one another, communing in fellowship and friendship – we are blessed to find God's power over all that we may fear.

### *A Prayer*

*Lord, thank you for the power of relationships and fellowship. Thank you for the people who walk alongside me in my times of fear and for the times when you have placed me in a position to do the same for my Brothers and Sisters. As I confront my fears today, big or small, known or unexpected, personal or shared, I ask that you yourself will walk with me and comfort me, along with others whom you have placed in my life intentionally for this moment. And as I walk alongside others, I pray that you would empower me with strength, wisdom, and compassion to be a comfort to them. Amen.*

# Day Nine: Honesty
🎧 *Suggested Streaming: Oh My Soul by Casting Crowns*

"Honesty" is one of the easiest words in the English language to understand, and yet, one of the most complex to grasp and tempting to dishonor. As I walked toward an absolutely breathtaking sunrise this morning, this song issued a timely call for total, cards-on-the-table, bare-naked honesty. I thought to myself, if this place – in perfect solitude, communing with God under the stunning beauty of his creation – is not a sanctuary, a safe place where I can be honest, then surely no such place exists here on earth. Honesty though, is a loaded and complicated word. It is an ideal, a practice, a call to live fully into who we are (including our brokenness), knowing that we are saved not by our words or deeds, but by the unconditional love of our sacrificial Savior.

While they are certainly related, I tend to distinguish honesty from truth. Truth is binary, rooted in the absolute. Something is either true or untrue, factual or fictional, accurate or inaccurate. The Bible gives us clear guidance about truth and lies. Jesus himself addresses the nature and origin of lies in John 8:42-47, where we find him telling the Jewish people of the devil's propensity for deceit, exclaiming that, "He was a murderer from the beginning, not holding to the truth for there is no truth in him. When he lies, he speaks his native language, for he is a liar and the father of lies (John 8:44)." On the other hand, we also know the familiar and infinitely comforting statement Jesus makes when he proclaims, "I am the way, the truth, and the life. No one comes to the Father except through me (John 14:6)." The juxtaposition of these two statements – holding them in the same breath – paints a picture of how important truthfulness is in shaping who we are. Jesus doesn't just call the devil a liar, but a _murderer_; and at the same time, Jesus, who _is truth_ is also _life_, and is the key to our eternal salvation. In this way, truth becomes a very real life or death proposition.

Truth may be black-and-white, but honesty is what gives truth its real depth and meaning. Honesty is about going deep – to the fullest extent of our truth – and embracing the flaws, shortcomings, and imperfections of our humanity. Fortunately, we have the opportunity to bring those imperfections to a God who understands

17

intimately the trials of being fully human. Jesus became entirely human, and "Because he himself suffered when he was tempted, he is able to help those who are being tempted (Hebrews 2:18)." But in order to be helped in our temptations, we must be willing to own them. Those we feel, those we fight, those we succumb to, and those we hide from. To be honest is to pretend nothing. When we bring ourselves to God in sheer honesty, we acknowledge, accept, and live into our humanity, our brokenness, and our sins, and in doing so, we confess our need for his saving grace.

That kind of honesty is hard to come by in a world that encourages us daily to hide our vulnerabilities and imperfections, and only ever to display the very best, varnished versions of ourselves. We needn't bother with that kind of window-dressing when we approach the throne of God though, because as the psalmist wrote, "Lord, you have searched me and known me. You know when I sit down and when I stand up; you understand my thoughts from far away. You observe my travels and my rest; you are aware of all my ways (Psalm 139:1-3)". God sees us, fully, entirely, completely, *honestly*, so we can embrace who we are and know beyond all doubt that despite all of it, we are fully loved. That kind of honesty, and that kind of love, is truly, deeply powerful.

### *A Prayer*

*Father, thank you for inviting me to your alter as I am. Entirely as I am. I pray that you would grant me faith to bring my whole self to you, that I may pretend nothing in your presence. In your abundant mercy, please forgive me for my sins, and in your abundant love and grace, please guide me along righteous paths moving forward. Lord, search me. Search my heart, see my motives, know my desires, and help me to align them to your will. Amen.*

# *Day Ten: Breaking Down, Building Up*
🎧 *Suggested Streaming: New Wine by Hillsong Worship*

"Senseless" suffering – or what we perceive as senseless – is heartbreaking. The suffering we cannot reconcile, does not make sense, and from which there is no perceptible relief or end in sight. The timeless challenge, "why do bad things happen to good people?" reminds us of our ceaseless need to somehow justify suffering. But maybe it is not the cause that justifies the means, but the outcome. Maybe it is not a question of whether we deserve to suffer (because if we're honest, the truth is we do), but a question of what change does our heart require? The process of changing, after all, is always hard. This morning's song brings that truth to bear in a poetic metaphor of pressing – *crushing* – grapes in order to make new wine. So often the process of creating something wonderful is, itself, anything but.

As we approach our own suffering and the suffering we see all around us, perhaps the question is not what did we do to deserve this, but rather, how will God use this? The Bible is brimming with stories and parables of destructive, painful, heart-wrenching suffering that inspired real change – changes that were absolutely essential for those individuals (or in some cases, all of mankind) to thrive. In the Old Testament, we find accounts of people who fit our more comfortable interpretation of how suffering ought to be administered – through a system of justice that demands one to reap what he has sown. Certainly, the story of Noah and the flood is evidence of this, of the ways in which God was forced by humanity's sinful nature to destroy the world in order to redeem it (Genesis 5:1 – 9:29). Another shining and familiar example is the suffering and exile of the Jews who repeatedly disobeyed their Lord until finally being made to wander in the wilderness, being denied entry to the Promised Land which would be given to their descendants (Numbers 14). These stories seem to pass the comfortable, if arbitrary, "fairness" test we subconsciously cling to, although it is the very same test we readily abandon in evaluating our own sinful natures.

Fortunately, we do not live in an Old Testament world in which a generation must be culled for its posterity to be redeemed. We live in the comfort, mercy, and undeserved grace of the New Covenant. With Jesus seated at the right hand of the Father, we know that the price for our sin has already been paid in full. Jesus promised that in this life we will experience trouble, suffering, and pain (John 16:33), but we can endure that pain knowing it is not redemptive, but restorative, not punitive, but purifying.

In John chapter 15, Jesus describes the pain we endure as being akin to the branches of a vine as it is pruned. Branches that bear no fruit must be cut away and discarded, but even the branches that do bear fruit require pruning. Even good vines need to be cut, their branches scarred, in order for the branches to thrive and abide more completely within the vine. This purifying grace is foretold by the prophet Malachi, who spoke of the Lord as the "refiner's fire" – a fire that is kindled and carefully controlled to bring out the best and most precious beauty of gold and silver without consuming or tarnishing them (Malachi 3:2-3).

We have all endured suffering – from the kind that mildly frustrates our minds to the kind that irreparably shatters our hearts – but through it all, we can take comfort in knowing that we are like silver refined in the flames of pain and trials, like branches pruned by the sharp blades of loss and heartache, like grapes crushed into fine new wine. And trusting in the careful hand of the refiner, the gardener, the vintner, our Father, we know that what is built back up will be more perfect, more mature, and much stronger than what was broken down.

### *A Prayer*

*Heavenly Father, it comes easily and naturally for me to thank you in prosperity and comfort, but today, I thank you equally – or even more so – for the trials, challenges, and losses you have set before me. I thank you for the ways you have grown and rebuilt me, and for the ways in which you continue to refine my heart. Help me to see you at work in my pain and suffering, and the pain and suffering all around me; and even when I can't see you clearly within those struggles, strengthen my faith to know that you are there and that you will use this for my good. Amen.*

# Day Eleven: Burdens

🎧 *Suggested Streaming: Burdens by Jamie Kimmett*

Whenever I wrestle with the idea of real surrender, it is usually in the context of control and direction, but Jesus also calls us to surrender our broken hearts, our stresses, our fears, the pressures we feel, and the pain we endure. He calls us to lay down all of our baggage, then turn and walk away from it. This morning the lyrics playing as I watched the darkness break into daylight were exactly what I needed to hear – and what I suspect many of us need to hear: that when we are on the brink of collapse and feel as though the world is crumbling around us, we are invited, welcomed, even beckoned to lay our burdens down at our Savior's feet. Every. Single. One.

When I listen to this song, I envision myself carrying literal suitcases, packages, boxes, and crates filled to the brim, heavy laden with the concerns of my heart. Some are filled with my sins and transgressions, some with my worries for my loved ones, financial stresses, work expectations, dreams and ambitions for the future, my many shortcomings, ways that I have failed to act when action was needed, things I have failed to say when words were wanted, compassion I have not extended, generosity I have withheld, all of my fears, trepidations, hesitations, and uncertainties. I carefully stack the boxes in my mind until the tower is unfathomably and overwhelmingly high. As I catalog these burdens in my mind, each box I stack recalls to memory another, and so I keep adding and adding.

When we do this, we quickly find the weight of our baggage is unbearable, the burden too great for our small shoulders. As we begin to feel crushed by our determination to personally bear the entire load, we may begin to wonder where exactly we are carrying them to? How often have we toted our baggage along with us – into our marriages, our friendships, our parenting, our work, and even our leisure – and how often have we allowed them to weigh our spirits down? How often have we fixed our eyes on the contents of each heavy box – or worse, on the collective whole of the entire stack – and become frozen with fear, wept with sorrow, rebelled with anger, or panicked with overwhelming anxiety? In those moments (and hopefully long before them), we are invited, just as the song beckons, to lay our burdens down at the cross, and to fully commend them into the care of the only one who is truly able to tend to them. Jesus himself issues the invitation, "Come to me, all you who are weary and burdened, and I will give you rest. Take my yoke upon you and learn from me, for I am gentle and humble in heart, and you will find rest for your souls. For my yoke is easy and my burden is light (Matthew 11:28-30)." In a similar way, the psalmist also assures us, saying, "Cast your cares on the Lord, and he will sustain you (Psalm 55:22)".

Paul instructed the Philippians in much the same way, urging them, "Do not be anxious about anything, but in everything, by prayer and petition, with thanksgiving, present your requests to God (Philippians 4:6)." It particularly strikes me that Paul doesn't compel us to bring only the really heavy, really tricky, really hard burdens to God. He doesn't say to bring our top 3, or, if we're honest, the minor ones that we don't mind God meddling with…we are to bring everything. We are to bring the entire contents of our hearts and minds, everything that weighs on us or pulls us in one direction or the other, everything that makes us question or causes us to pause, everything that instills doubt or embodies fear. Everything. And we are to leave it there, at the cross, trusting the Son of God to carry it forward for us. Rather than imagining the tall, looming, intimidating towers of our worries, shortcomings, doubts, temptations, and fears, we can instead imagine ourselves – box by overflowing box – handing them to our Savior who easily, willingly, and joyfully assumes their burden for us and exchanges his easy yoke and light burden in return.

### A Prayer

*Thank you, Jesus, for taking my burdens from me and for lightening the weight of this heavy load I carry. Lord, you know every piece of baggage I have stored away, every worry I entertain, every outcome I fear, every guilt I hide, sorrow I feel, and concern I hold – even the ones I try to downplay, conceal, or ignore. Please soften my heart today, my heart which is determined to carry these burdens on my own, and turn me instead toward you and your open invitation to lay them down and walk away. Amen.*

# Day Twelve: Perfect Love

🎧 *Suggested Streaming: Who You Say I Am by Hillsong Worship and You Say by Lauren Daigle*

Deepening our relationship with God is a journey of intentionality and curiosity, and I have found that much of my curiosity is fueled by how I am led to seek out God, to relate to him, and to live in the ways he calls me to live. Today, two songs stirred my curiosity about the Father's heart and his perceptions of me: Who You Say I Am by Hillsong Worship, and shortly after, You Say, Lauren Daigle. The combination of these two songs enticed my mind to wonder, "What exactly does God think of me?"

In a world of constant, total access, it's easy to feel vulnerable and exposed at times. We find ourselves constantly wondering how we are perceived, and whether those perceptions are a true depiction. In the world, the impressions we make, and the impressions we form of each other, are often only based on a small fraction of the real story. We see each other superficially, and often through a self-curated lens that allows us to edit and filter what we show the world. We make assumptions and judgements based on each other's actions without knowing their intentions. We decide who to love and how to love them without all the information, and we let that information shape, influence, or compromise how we love.

Author and Pastor Timothy Keller describes love in this way: "To be loved but not known is comforting but superficial. To be known and not loved is our greatest fear. But to be fully known and truly loved is a lot like being loved by God. It is what we need more than anything." What an amazing and humbling thought – to be *fully* known, all of our best and worst intentions, the deepest pains, greatest joys, our strongest achievements and most egregious transgressions, our visible actions and deeds, and the invisible motives of our hearts and minds – all of it in full daylight, all of our cards on the table, completely exposed…and yet to be *truly loved* in both the splendor and brokenness of it all. That kind of love is rare, if not impossible, on earth because the inclination to doubt ourselves and each other is deeply engrained in our nature. We doubt our ability to love, we question each other's motives, we wonder and speculate about our own goodness, and struggle to feel fully known or fully loved. If we set all that noise aside though, the real question is what does our Father, Creator, and Savior think of us?

To understand the depth of God's love for us, we have to go back to the very beginning – Genesis 1:27, "God created man in his own image; he created him in the image of God." We are created in Imago Dei – the image of God – because he so deeply loves us that he chose to reflect his own nature within and through us. He created us to be the channel through which his plans and his purposes are actualized, and by creating us in his image, he endowed us with the capacity to do so. Because we reflect the creator himself, God knows that we are capable of meeting every challenge to which we are called, not because of our own abilities, but because his abilities are brought to bear through us.

Not only did God create us thoughtfully and deliberately in his image, but he also takes tremendous pride in that creation. He says, "I have called you by name; you are mine (Isaiah 43:16)." And because we are his, God loves us with the kind of perfect love Pastor Keller described. Our all-seeing, all-knowing, all-powerful Father knows every good and bad deed we have performed, idea and thought we have entertained, desire we have courted, and instinct we have felt. The God who knows fully the true nature and content of our hearts loves us so completely that he sent his son to die in order for us to be reconciled with him. Regardless of our shortcomings and our transgressions, "God proves his own love for us in that while we were still sinners, Christ died for us (Romans 5:8)."

One of the most well-known verses in all of the Bible is John 3:16: "For God so loved the world, he gave his one and only Son, so that everyone who believes in him will not perish but will have eternal life." That is a love that is hard for me to fathom. I know the heartbreak of losing a son, the pain of seeing your child hurting, and the deep urge to protect your child from anything that might harm them. The truth that God loves me (and you!) so much that he allowed his son to die and did not shield him from pain, because he knew that through his son's death he would be reconciled with us – that is a love that defies all comprehension. Rather than try to understand love that perfect, despite all of our imperfections, and rather than striving to deserve it, which we never can, we must instead seek to simply accept it. We accept it gratefully, because we know we don't deserve it; humbly, because we know the price that was paid for it; freely, because we were created to receive it; and repeatedly, because it is renewed each and every day. And having accepted it, we must also seek to share it, as Jesus bids us to do: "Love one another. Just as I have loved you, you are also to love one another (John 13:34)."

### *A Prayer*

*Thank you, Father, for knowing me fully and loving me completely. Thank you for the beautiful and humbling truth that I am created in your image, bearing your nature, and possessing your ability to receive and give love. Help me today Lord to accept the love you offer to me, just as a child relishes and relies on the love of his parents. Please also help me to share your love through my own actions and relationships, and lead me to be an example of Christ's love today. Amen.*

# Day Thirteen: Brokenness

🎧 *Suggested Streaming: Scars by I Am They*

Once again, God tells me clearly that he sees me, as I was greeted this morning with light sprawling spectacularly across the horizon and the song playing over my headphones spoke of the hopeful promise of a new sunrise. As I watched, I thought to myself how amazing it is when that sun breaks out over the horizon each day, and suddenly everything about the dark night is washed away in the color and light. Sometimes we have to be on the other side of the darkness to really understand, and even appreciate, what it was all about. In this song, I Am They takes it one step further by proclaiming that because of that appreciation, they wouldn't trade their most painful experiences for anything.

I thought about this, and if I'm being completely honest, all I could do was ask, "Really?? You wouldn't trade them for *anything*? *Nothing*? Why not??" I know we're not supposed to say that, we're supposed to have no regrets, right? But I confess, I would trade my pain – absolutely and without hesitation. I would give back my greatest, deepest, most hurt-filled moments, and I would probably give back a thousand smaller pains along the way as well. I would trade my darkest experiences and darkest tragedies – In. A. Heartbeat. Happy, easily, and without question.

But then the song continues on to explain that in our brokenness is often where we find God, and that he uses our struggles to bring about his good will. For that, the song proclaims, we can be grateful for the scars we bear. As I consider this, I remember that God does not cause pain or sorrow, but he will use it. He will use it in ways that defy all understanding. When Joseph's brothers came to him to beg forgiveness for how they had mistreated and abused him – to the point of selling him as a slave and telling their father he died – and yet he gave it freely, saying, "You intended to do harm to me, but God intended it for good to accomplish what is now being done…" (Genesis 50:20). Even in the most extreme scars we experience, there is a larger fabric that our lives weave into.

I don't know if I am grateful for my scars – in some ways I think I am – but I am absolutely grateful that it isn't up to me to give them back. If we can bear our scars willingly, or at least obediently, then we can lift them to the

Lord to shape who we are and what those scars will mean. We can strive to follow the example of our Savior, who, on the Mount of Olives made the same petition we make in the hardest moments of life on earth. "Father, if you are willing, take this cup from me." Of course, Jesus continues where we tend to stop, and he adds, "Yet not my will, but yours be done." (Like 22:42). It makes me wonder, what if the Lord's will had not been carried out at Cavalry? What if He did indeed take the cup from his son and spared him the cross? Our fallen world would be without hope. But He didn't. For God so loved the world that he gave his one and only son, that whoever believes in him shall not perish but have eternal life (John 3:16). God's will, his plan, his work is for a greater purpose and a greater good than we can begin to fathom. This has been true since the beginning of creation, it was true when Jesus was crucified, it is true in our lives today. Were it up to most of us, we would give back many cups, but God has a different – better – plan, and he is faithful to realize it.

### *A Prayer*

*Father, as hard as this is and strange as it seems, we thank you for our suffering. We thank you for the confidence you give us to face our struggles, for the resolve and strength you give us in the midst of the battles, and for the peace and wisdom you offer us on the other side. Help me today to remember that you have already seen my victory and have already put plans in place to secure it. Even though that victory may be different from what I am hoping for or envisioning, help me to know that my scars have meaning and that bearing them makes me stronger. Amen.*

# Day Fourteen: Waiting

🎧 *Suggested Streaming: Even So Come by Kristian Stanfill*

This morning's lyrics brought to mind my most hated of all activities: waiting. The hardest part of waiting, at least for me, is dealing with the ambiguities and uncertainties of it. What am I waiting for? When will it come? How can I prepare? And of course…why is taking so long??

In those seasons when all of those questions are swirling, and when they feel unlikely to be answered anytime soon, it's easy to feel a little stuck. Our frenetic work and worry starts to feels a bit like a hamster wheel – running, running, and running, but in the end, never actually getting anywhere. This morning as I prepare myself to step back onto that proverbial wheel, the voice of Kristian Stanfill breaks through to remind me that there is something far greater we are waiting for. Greater than the phone call we are waiting to receive. Greater than the opportunities we are waiting to realize. Greater than the battles we are waiting to end. Greater than all the financial, family, friendship, work, and world questions we are eagerly awaiting for answers for.

While waiting may feel like its own special kind of suffering, with all of its doubt and impatience, Paul reminds us in his letter to the Roman Church, "For I consider that the sufferings of this present time are not worth comparing with the glory that is going to be revealed to us. For the creation eagerly awaits with anticipation for God's son to be revealed (Romans 8:18-19)." Revelation tells us that when the Son does return, there will be a new heaven and a new earth. That God will dwell with us wiping away every tear, and death, grief, crying, and pain will no longer exist (Revelation 21:1-4). Now that certainly seems like a promise and a hope worth waiting for – and we know that God is faithful to keep his promises, so why do we still feel so unsettled? So restless? So impatient?

Perhaps it stems from the fact that while we have great hope for what is to come, and by that I mean both the return of Christ as well as the infinitely smaller concerns of our many unanswered questions, we can't yet see it. We can't imagine that future world yet, we can't wrap our heads around the possibilities it may hold, and so we allow ourselves to become fearful of the worst scenarios rather than eager for the best. Of course, Paul had an answer for this as well, and his letter continued, "Now in this hope we were saved, but hope that is seen is not hope, because who hopes for what he sees? Now if we hope for what we do not see, we eagerly wait for it with patience (Romans 8:24-25)."

I am particularly intrigued by Paul's call to wait both eagerly *and* with patience. I think the only way to accomplish both of these tasks is to be certain – for we can wait eagerly and patiently if, and only if, we also wait *expectantly*. When we are sure of what is coming, and we are certain that what is coming will be good, a switch flips and suddenly we go from waiting and worrying to planning and preparing. In knowing that God is coming, we prepare ourselves by living in ways he has called us to live. We prepare by sharing his love and his word with others so they can be prepared too. We prepare by praying, and by turning over all of our fears and worries in acknowledgement that he is and will always be in control.

In the same way, as we wait here on earth for resolution, answers, guidance, comfort, direction, purpose, and peace, we can do so expectantly – knowing that he is working all things together for our good (Romans 8:28). Because of this, we can wait, not passively or helplessly, but with purpose and in preparation. We don't have to become paralyzed by the unknown, nor run in place in a seemingly interminable pattern. Because we know who our God is, that he is good and almighty, and because we know he is coming again to rid us of all our suffering, we can take all of our doubt, uncertainty, and frenetic hurry, and we can leave it at the foot of the cross. In so doing, we can confidently echo the words of the prophet Micah, "But I will look to the Lord, I will wait for the God of my salvation. My God will hear me. (Micah 7:7)."

### *A Prayer*

*Heavenly Father, thank you for your perfect plans, to execute your perfect will, in your perfect timing. I pray that you would instill patience in my heart as I wait for you. Please fortify my resiliency and help me to see how you are preparing me in this season. Through your Holy Spirit, help me to wait, not doubtingly or anxiously, but expectantly, for the good plans I know you have and which I may not even yet imagine. Amen.*

# Day Fifteen: Greater Things

🎧 *Suggested Streaming: Trust in You by Lauren Daigle*

The head pastor of our church closes each of his sermons with a familiar and gracefully worded benediction from Ephesian 3:20-21, "Now to him who is able to do immeasurably more than all we can ask or imagine, according to his will at work within us – to him be the glory in the church and in Christ Jesus to all generations, now and forever. Amen." This scripture is recalled to my mind every time I hear the song Lauren Daigle sang into my headphones this morning about wanting all the Lord has willed for us, and accepting nothing less.

I want nothing less than what you have planned. Nothing less than what you wish for me. Nothing less than what you are capable of bringing about for me. Nothing less than the greater – indeed, greatest – things you have in store. What a powerful and bold stance! But, how often do we instead pray for God to come alongside our "good" plans? To endorse them, rubber-stamp them, or even to actively set them in motion? How often do we pray for what we want because it is the best-case scenario that we, in our microscopically limited scope of reference, can imagine? Rather than lift up our worries and fears in prayer, we lift up our solutions. Rather than ask for deliverance, we ask the Almighty Lord for his tacit compliance.

Yet Ephesians tells us that he is able to do more – immeasurably more – not only than all we can ask, propose, suggest, demand, expect, or require, but all that we can *imagine*. I don't know about you, but I have a pretty vivid imagination…the kind that can run clean off the tracks and straight into the deep end of who-knows-where. Even so, when I look back on the greatest blessings of my life, the most powerful turning points, tenderest moments, most joyful celebrations, and the most pivotal opportunities, they all have one thing in common: I never saw them coming. Each of those blessings, though they did not always feel so, was something I never could have imagined, and they manifested along courses I never could have plotted.

Just a few chapters earlier in Paul's letter to the Ephesians, he prays "that the eyes of your heart may be enlightened so that you may know what is the hope of his calling, what is the wealth of his glorious inheritance in the saints, and what is the immeasurable greatness of his power toward us who believe, according to the mighty working of his strength (Ephesians 1:18-20)." We are deeply, truly, and fully loved by a Father with infinite wisdom and immeasurable ability, so why do we tend to limit and confine his authority by asking him to go along with our will? How much more powerful would it be if we could just lay all of our cards out on the table and simply say, "Lord, I have no idea what you're going to do with this, but, I trust you. Take it all. Please."? That is exactly what Hezekiah did when he received word of the destruction and devastation caused by the Assyrian kings. Hezekiah didn't petition the Lord to ratify or endorse his plan nor did he lay out a strategy or a campaign for victory. He simply "spread it out [the message] before the Lord (Isaiah 37:14)" and he prayed, "Now Lord our God, deliver us from his hand, so that all the kingdoms of the earth may know that you, Lord, are the only God (Isaiah 37:20)." When we start talking to God about the deepest needs of our hearts, anchored by his goodness, glory, and power – and when we leave the means, the "how", out of it – that's when the imagination of the all-powerful, almighty God comes to bear.

Honestly, at the end of the day, why would we want to set the strategy anyway? We have unlimited, unrestricted access to the one who turned water in to wine (John 2:1-11), raised a child from the dead (Luke 7:11-18), stilled a raging storm (Matthew 8:23-27), opened the eyes of the blind (Matthew 9:27-31), fed thousands of people from five loaves of bread and two fish (Matthew 14:15-21)…and the list goes on. How could our plans, our solutions, and our ideas ever be better than his? The one who breaks through every thread of the fabric of our imaginations. The one who plans greater things for us than we can begin to comprehend. They can't – pure and simple. Rather than try to assert our own flawed wisdom, let us strive to be more like Hezekiah, laying it all out in front of the Lord and asking him – gratefully and with anticipation – to chart the path forward. And then, let us follow that path faithfully.

### A Prayer

*God, thank you for being the ultimate planner, creator, and course charter. Today, please help me to get out of your way so that I may never again settle for less than what you have intended. Lord, you know the challenges I face and the struggles that are on my heart. I lay them all before you now, stripped of my own ideas, plans, intentions, and preferences, and I ask you to guide me to overcome them. You have already seen each of these battles from the victory. Lord, lead the way. Amen.*

# Day Sixteen: Joy Anew

🎧 *Suggested Streaming: Come as You Are by Crowder*

As a recovering English major, aspiring writer, and – let's be honest – someone who probably just talks too much, words hold a very special place in my heart. I love the versatility of words, and the infinite ways our perceptions and interpretations change based on the words we hear, say, read, learn, and understand. Consider for a moment a word like "love". You may be reading this as someone who is in love, or someone who is loved, someone who loves their children, spouse, parents, friends, dogs, or white chocolate peppermint ice cream. How mind boggling it is to think of the broad spectrum of things we can reasonably apply the word "love" to. If the word can be ascribed to everything from God's perfect, unfailing, unconditional love for us all the way to my (admittedly absurd) love of marshmallows, then clearly context matters.

I wonder if the same can be said for the word "joy". Often, we think of joy as synonymous with happiness, but in doing so, have we diminished the truth of this powerful word? This, I wondered, as I listened to Crowder sing about the joy that comes with each morning and the assurance that Heaven can heal every sorrow. As I think in particular about these daily sunrise journeys, I am struck by how joy truly does come in the morning. David wrote, "Sing to the Lord, you his faithful ones, and praise his holy name. For his anger lasts only a moment, but his favor a lifetime. Weeping may stay overnight, but there is joy in the morning (Psalm 30:4-5)."

We can relate to David, for how often have we found our hearts changed when we wake up after a hard night? Whether it is a night of deep grief, pain, loss, and suffering, or simply the end of a tedious and frustrating day, the morning often brings renewed joy. This is not to say we all wake up happy and our pain is gone, but that we often wake up better understanding the pain that felt incomprehensible just hours before. Joy in our hearts is neither pleasure about our circumstances nor even acceptance of them. To me, the joy that comes in the morning – after a night of grief and sorrow, and after a time of reflection, lament, and rest (exhaustion-induced though that rest may be) – that kind of joy is the realization and belief that good will come. Joy in our hearts transcends our circumstances, it is constant and doesn't waiver like temporal happiness, fleeting delight, or temporary satisfaction. It is steadfast in all circumstances, and it is renewed day by day, morning by morning.

The second part of Crowder's poetic lyrics remind us that although we are sinners, God heals all of our sorrows. This truth helps us to live into that renewed joy every day and assures us that joy endures even when our bodies, minds, relationships, and hearts may be broken. First, and importantly, this song reminds us of the origin and undeniable root of our suffering – sin. God did not intend for our world, his creation, to be filled with suffering. God created man Imago Dei – in his image, in his likeness, in his nature. The real root of both the suffering we experience and the suffering we inflict is the constant temptation to choose sin over goodness. Yet, no matter how deep, there truly is no sorrow that Heaven can't heal. Jesus redeemed our sins and now we can look joyfully toward Heaven, where God will once again dwell with humanity. Where he will wipe away every tear from our eyes. Death, grief, crying, and pain will be no more (Revelations 21:4). Because we know this truth, we can join the psalmist in rejoicing, "My flesh and my heart may fail, but God is the strength of my heart and my portion forever (Psalm 73:26)."

### *A Prayer*

*Heavenly Father, thank you for the promise of your eternal joy. Please help me remember as David proclaimed, that while my pain may last overnight, and although the night may feel interminable, that joy comes in the morning. Help me to be comforted by the inexplicable peace that only you can offer, and comfort me with the certain knowledge that your Kingdom will eliminate all the pain and suffering that this world can sometimes bring. Help me to rest my heart in your joy, no matter my circumstances. Amen.*

# Day Seventeen: Seen

🎧 *Suggested Streaming: Rescue by Lauren Daigle*

I am an introvert by nature, so being on my own is often comforting, re-energizing, even enjoyable; but being by one's self and being alone can be two very different things. Sometimes feeling alone has nothing at all to do with who or how many we're surrounded by. Sometimes it is a feeling of being lost, grasping, waiting, or wishing for something that no one else understands. It is a feeling of being misunderstood, unknown, unseen. But we are never truly alone, never truly unseen, never hidden nor forgotten, nor out of reach from God's rescue.

Even those of us who are blessed, as I am grateful to be, by a loving family, dear friends, welcoming congregations, and warm, embracing neighbors experience maddening, heart-wrenching loneliness sometimes. At some point, the circumstances of our lives will cause us to feel isolated or abandoned. Maybe we grieve a loss in unexpected ways, or we feel disappointment when we are supposed to rejoice, we take a risk when the world demands caution, or we play it safe when the world encourages boldness. Whatever the circumstances, being out on the ledge alone is a terrifying feeling.

The fear entrenched in that feeling is exactly why the message that we are never hidden, never forgotten, never alone, is so important. The Bible is filled with references to the countless ways God watches over us – individually, knowingly, intentionally, and constantly. "The eyes of the Lord are in every place, watching the evil and the good (Proverbs 15:3)."; "For his eyes are on the ways of man, and he sees all his steps (Job 34:21)."; The Lord looks from Heaven, He sees all the sons of man; from his dwelling place he looks out on all the inhabitants of the earth (Psalm 33:13-14)."; and the list goes on and on.

We know that the Lord our God watches all and sees all because of his genuine love and care for his children; but in our darkest, loneliest, most deserted moments, do we remember his constant company and his omniscient sight? Hagar did. The badly mistreated slave of Abram and Sarai had fled her masters' home and was alone, not to mention pregnant and fearful. While we may not be able to relate to Hagar's situation exactly, she was hurt, confused, sad, and desperately uncertain of what her future held – all feelings we understand intimately. The Lord not only saw Hagar in her moment of need, but he called her by name. He knew her situation, felt her pain, and he guided her and provided for her. During that encounter, Hagar names the Lord as, "El roi" – the God who sees me. (Genesis 16:13). A similar story unfolded about two thousand years later when Jesus encountered the Samaritan woman at the well in Sychar. That Jesus spoke to her, and spoke kindly, would have been admirable enough, given the cultural norms of the time in which Jews did not associate with Samaritans, but he did much more than that. He showed that he knew her. He knew her deeds, her story, he understood her needs, and he provided for her by revealing himself as the Messiah – the living water. (John 4:1-26).

Through these examples, and in countless others in the Bible and in our day-to-day lives, we can be certain that God absolutely sees us. He knows us by name (John 10:3), indeed, he knows the number of hairs on our heads (Matthew 10:30). When you feel alone, forgotten, lost, marginalized, set aside, or hidden entirely, remember that "The Lord will watch over your coming and going, both now and forevermore (Psalm 121:8)." And as he watches, just as he knew Hagar's name, he knows your name; just as he knew the Samaritan woman's story, he knows yours. Even when we can't fully understand or articulate our needs, or when we hide them behind masks we've crafted for ourselves or armor we've donned around our hearts, God sees us. "We do not know what we ought to pray for, but the Spirit himself intercedes for us with groans that words cannot express. (Romans 8:26)." We are never hidden – we are seen, we are known, we are provided for, and we are loved.

### *A Prayer*

*Father, thank you for your omnipresence and omniscience – for being present and here with me, for knowing my story intimately, for knowing my needs completely, and for seeing me even when I feel hidden and alone. Lord, please help me to trust that you are listening, and that you know the needs written on my heart even when I can't form the words on my lips. Please comfort me, and all those who feel lonely, with the knowledge and faith that you are with us – always. Amen.*

# Day Eighteen: Grace and Fear

*⌕ Suggested Streaming: Amazing Grace (hymn)*

Like most nights, my family sat down for dinner last night and together we recited a familiar prayer, asking the Lord to bless our meal. At the end of the prayer, as we filled our plates, I asked my son if he ever thinks about the meaning of prayers we recite from memory. As we broke down the blessing, line by line, I could see a new appreciation light up his eyes. How many times has the familiarity of praying words we know by heart caused us to miss – or forget – their sacred meaning? When we recite the Lord's Prayer, do we pause to comprehend that God provides in abundance and without hesitation by giving us our daily bread? When we affirm our faith by the Apostle's Creed, do we pause in reverence that Jesus was crucified, died and was buried, that he descended into Hell, and that he rose again? Do we acknowledge that this sentence recalled from years of repetition actually changes everything?

These are the questions that struck me today as I approached the sunrise. Having watched the sunrise enough at this point to be dangerously close to falling into a routine, the most familiar song of all-time streams across my headphones and I catch myself mindlessly – almost out of habit – mouthing the words, "'twas grace that taught my heart to fear, and grace my fear released. How precious did that grace appear the hour I first believed (Amazing Grace, John Newton)." How many times have we sung these words? In church, around a campfire, in a rocking chair, at a graveside…the words are forged in many of our hearts, engraved in our souls, fortified in our memories, and yet today, I realized that they make absolutely no sense! How can grace teach us to fear and also release our fears? How are we to be "God-fearing" and also "fear not"?

In my mind, fear has everything to do with power. We are afraid of something or someone because we perceive that it has power over us. We fear illness that has power over our bodies, we fear the loss of our job for the power it has over our finances or our sense of purpose, we fear the loss of loved ones, dangerous weapons, careless friends, apathetic politicians, snakes and spiders, all in deference to the power we believe they wield. By this definition,

35

it is not only natural, but expected that we ought to fear the Lord. Who is more powerful? When God spoke to the Israelites to impart his commandments, it was with thunder and lightning and mountain smoke – and the Israelites trembled with fear (Exodus 20:18). Even before that, God sent plagues of blood, frogs, gnats, flies, pestilent livestock, boils, hail, locusts, darkness, and death to Egypt to inspire obedient fear in the heart of the Pharaoh (Exodus 7-12). And before that, the Lord flooded the earth for 150 days, wiping out the wicked human race, save for Noah and his family (Genesis 7). Clearly our Lord is one to be feared, and certainly, as the song proclaims, he has taught our hearts to fear.

How then does the one who taught us to fear also *release* us from fear? If the foundation of fear is anchored by a thing's power, then our ability not to fear must rest in its nature. We don't necessarily fear power in and of itself, but rather, we fear what we believe will come of that power. It's true that God is almighty, all-powerful, but God's nature is also true and perfect love; and "There is no fear in love. Instead, perfect love drives out fear because fear is punishment (1 John 4:18)." The perfect love and sacrifice of Jesus redeemed us – fully, completely, and eternally – so the punishment we deserve and are compelled to fear has been replaced by, as the song declares, God's amazing grace.

If we know the true heart of God, his nature, we know that he is good. References to God's goodness are found all throughout scripture, but perhaps most clearly in Exodus when God came down in a cloud at Mount Sinai, and as the Egyptians trembled with fear, he proclaimed his nature, "The Lord – the Lord is a compassionate and gracious God, slow to anger and abounding in faithful love and truth, maintaining faithful love to a thousand generations, forgiving iniquity, rebellion, and sin. (Exodus 34:6-7)" In the new covenant, "God proves his love for us, in that while we were still sinners, Christ died for us (Romans 5:8)." We are saved by *amazing*, astonishing, monumental grace through faith alone because of God's fundamentally good nature and abundant love (Ephesians 2:8), and because of that, we can confidently release our fears.

As I pause to think about the meaning of these words we have sung for decades, I recall a beloved book that beautifully illustrates this intersection of grace and fear. C.S. Lewis captures the dichotomy perfectly in *The Lion, the Witch, and the Wardrobe*. Upon learning that Aslan (the ruler of Narnia) is a lion, Susan asks if he is "quite safe?" and Mr. Beaver responds simply, "'Course he isn't safe. But he's good. He's the King." Like the lion, God represents the only thing so powerful that our hearts should fear it, and yet, because he is good, and because he is King, we need not.

### A Prayer

*All-powerful, almighty God, thank you for your amazing grace, and for being both fearful and good. Because of your nature, we worship and obey a God who is worthy of our fear but who loves us so abundantly and so perfectly that we can approach your throne of grace unafraid. Please continue to lead us each and every day as our good King and help me to follow and obey you as King in my own life. Help me to remember when lesser things create fear and worry in my heart, that you are in control and that all my fears may be released into your capable hands. Amen.*

# Day Nineteen: Contradictions, Complexities, Completeness

🎧 *Suggested Streaming: How Great is Our God by Chris Tomlin*

With the thought of a God who is both fearful and fear-relieving still nudging at my mind, this morning I began my journey thinking of the other seemingly contradictory, or maybe complimentary – but definitely complex – attributes of our God. Coincidently, I thought about these competing descriptions while both the moon and the sun hung together in the sky, and as Chris Tomlin's voice praised a God who is the Beginning and the End, and who is the Father, the Spirit, and the Son.

Wait…what? Like many Christians, I have heard, and dutifully recited versions of these two descriptors for so long, even reverently crossing my heart at the proclamation of the Holy Trinity, that I almost never pause to really think about them. But honestly, how can God be both the beginning *and* the end? How can he be the Father, *and* the Son, *and* the Spirit? And how is that moon still hanging perfectly above the rising sun?

Let's start with "beginning and the end". Jesus himself proclaims that he is the Alpha and the Omega, the first and the last, the beginning and the end (Revelation 22:13). The implication of this is important, because Christ is not only the beginning and the end, but also everything in between. In order to embody both ends of the spectrum, he must embody the entirety of the spectrum. He is the spectrum. He is time itself. There is a constancy and an endurance in this that allows our faith to be anchored in that which is steadfast, unchanging, and eternal. The Apostle John tells us, "In the beginning was the Word and the Word was God. He was with God in the beginning. All things were created through him, and apart from him not one thing was created that has been created. In him was the life, and that was the light of man. (John 1:1-4). Our God precedes "the beginning" – he has always been – and he is "the end" – he will always be. Because of this fundamental truth, we can follow him faithfully and confidently, knowing he is not temporal, not fleeting, not contemporary. He is. And his power stands now as strongly as in the days of Noah, Abraham, Moses, and David. Along with this power, God's faithful love endures forever (Psalm 136), because he himself endures forever.

If the "beginning and the end" speaks to the enduring constancy of God, then the Trinity – the Godhead three in one – speaks to His relational nature. Far from being a contradiction, the truth that our Lord is Father, Spirit, and Son is a reflection of the completeness of our relationship with him. Through these identities, God invites us into a relationship that is fully sufficient for our needs. The Father is our creator – we are the clay and he is the potter, we are the work of his hands (Malachi 2:10). As our Father, God interacts with us as fathers do: molding us, training us to do what is right, what is good, teaching us to fear evil, rebuking us when we go astray, but always with enduring love, welcoming us back upon each and every one of our prodigal returns. What love the Father has given, that we should be called his children! (John 3:1).

The Son then is the God who we relate to because he relates to us. Through the incarnation of Jesus, "The Word became flesh and dwelt among us (John 1:14)." When God humbled himself to become flesh, he entered fully into our humanity and our brokenness. God as the Son – Jesus – experienced the pain and heartbreak of loss as he wept over the death of his friend Lazarus (John 11:35). He experienced anger, thrashing a whip and overturning tables in the temple when it was irreverently turned to a marketplace (John 2:13-16). He was tempted, and though he did not sin, he knows what it is to wrestle with the impulse to satisfy worldly desires (Matthew 4:1-11). Jesus experienced betrayal and rejection at the hands of those he loved (Luke 22:47-48; 54-62), and he cried out in fear, feeling abandoned and alone (Matthew 27:46). Because our God who is fully divine, humbled himself to also become fully human, he understands our pain in a real, intimate, been-there-done-that kind of way. We can bring our sadness, anger, temptation, loneliness, rejection, and fear to the Son because he too has experienced the brokenness of a fragile human heart. Most importantly, by his death, Jesus redeems us, making it possible for us to have a relationship with God in all three forms (John 14:6).

So if God the Father is our Creator, and God the Son is our Redeemer, then the Holy Spirit is our Counselor. After his resurrection, Jesus asked the Father to send another Counselor to be with his followers forever – the Spirit of Truth who remains in us and with us (John 14:15-16). This is important…the presence of the Holy Spirit in us *changes everything*. Because the Spirit of the God who raised Jesus from the dead lives in us, that same God also raises our mortal bodies to eternal life (Romans 8:11). An eternal life that starts now. Today. The Holy Spirit is with us now, here on earth, to guide how we think, how we act, how we live, and who we are *here on earth*. It allows our minds to transcend thoughts of selfishness and sin and instead encourages us to fix our thoughts on life and peace (Romans 8:5-6), which fundamentally shapes how we life in the world, how we treat each other, and how we treat ourselves. The Spirit, the Counselor, releases us from being slaves to our sins and from being beholden to our fears, because through its very presence, we are claimed – stamped, marked, certified, signed, sealed, delivered – as God's treasured, beloved child right now, today, on this side of Heaven (Romans 8:15-16).

Sometimes the words we use to describe God can leave us confused, grasping for adjectives and metaphors to describe that which is indescribable. Try as we might, semantics will always fall short of capturing a God who is eternal, time itself, creator, redeemer, and counselor, completely abundant, completely sufficient, and who claims us as his own. The beginning and the end. Alpha and Omega. Father. Spirit. Son.

## A Prayer

*Thank you Lord for all that you are, which is everything. Thank you for being all that we need, abundant not only in being, but also in love, mercy, provision, and grace. Please help me to remember today no matter what I face, it is nothing that your perfect and completely sufficient will can't handle. Thank you for your eternal and triune nature, that I can worship you as my Creator, Redeemer, and Counselor, knowing you have always been and will always be. Amen.*

# Day Twenty: Raise my Ebenezer

🎧 *Suggested Streaming: Come Thou Font of Every Blessing (hymn)*

Some days have a way of imprinting, carving, burning themselves into our hearts. For me, today is one such day. It was on this day many years ago that my world crumbled, and my faith along with it. It was the last day I held my son in my arms. The last day I kissed his face, held his tiny hand, swaddled him tightly in a soft, warm blanket. The last time I dreamed about his future or worried how we would get him through to that future.

You may not relate to this experience – indeed, I pray that you do not and never will – but perhaps you do know what it is to live through one of your very worst fears. If you are a parent, I'm sure you understand what I mean when I say that my son was the most wonderful and most terrifying thing to have ever changed my life. I spent the months leading up to his birth absolutely panicked. I was certain that I would be a bad parent. Convinced that we would not be able to make ends meet. Scared. Worried. Anxious. Doubtful. Unprepared. But the day he was born, all of the fear, all of the trepidation, all of the worry dissolved instantly. Or perhaps it didn't go away, but rather, it was replaced with a different kind of fear. It was no longer a fear driven by my own lacking abilities, but a deeper, almost primitive fear, driven by the powerful love that settles into a parent's heart. I wasn't afraid of being a "bad mom" anymore, I was afraid that I couldn't be the perfect mom, the abundant provider, the faultless leader, the shining example that this precious child deserved.

The day he died is a day that I have relived in slow-motion more times than I can count. The week that followed is a blurry, foggy memory which somehow culminated in a funeral service I can recall in glimpses, but that day… every second of it is etched into my brain in perfect detail. When my mind turns to those memories, I try also to remind myself that God has carried me, walked alongside me, pushed and pulled me, all this time. At a time when I felt – and still feel – helpless, I bring to mind the words of an old favorite hymn:

Sorrowing I shall be in spirit
Till released from flesh and sin
Yet from what I do inherit
Here thy praises I'll begin
Here I raise my Ebenezer
Here by Thy great help I've come
And I hope by Thy good pleasure
Safely to arrive at home
(Come Thou Font of Every Blessing, Robert Robinson)

This beautiful hymn offers permission to feel broken in this world, and also trust that we will be whole again in the next. That our spirit can sorrow, and that we can live fully into that pain without pretense, judgement, or shame. It is also a call to "raise our Ebenezer" and to remember how God has protected, supported, and loved us through every step of the journey here. The phrase comes from Samuel, who was determined to remind the Israelites of God's faithful protection, and he sought a reminder that would last not for a few hours or days, but for generations to come. When the Israelites were at their most desperate moment, perilously close to being attacked and easily defeated by the Philistines, Samuel prayed for God's protection. Although the Israelites had been prone to wander from their Lord and they consistently neglected their commitment to honor and glorify him, when they humbled themselves before him, professed their faith in his power, and affirmed their reliance on him, God came through. After God rescued them from the Philistines, Samuel offered a practical reminder of his faithfulness so that the Israelites would not turn from their Lord again. He lifted up a stone and called it "Ebenezer" ("stone of help" in Hebrew") and he placed it at the battle site, urging Israel to always remember, "Thus far has the Lord helped us (1 Samuel 7:12)."

In our darkest moments, and our brightest, and all those in between, the Lord has helped us. May we never doubt that he is also helping us now, and that he will forever, even when it's hard to imagine how. It can be easy to question God's presence when we're in our darkest valleys, but in the messiness and hurt of those moments, we can raise our Ebenezer, and remember that God has helped us – thus far, now, and forever. He is and will always be faithful.

### *A Prayer*

*God, I am grateful that you have been with me up to now, and that no matter what battles I face, you are with me still. You were honest with us that in this world we would encounter suffering, you have prepared me for it, and you gave me your Holy Spirit to guide and protect me through it all. Lord, you know the hurts on my heart, and I lift them all up to you now. Along with my sorrows, I raise my Ebenezer, and I remember that you are faithful forever. Please give me strength to endure until this battle is over, and please give me faith to know that you have already secured its victory. Amen.*

# Day Twenty-One: Surrender
🎧 *Suggested Streaming: With Lifted Hands by Ryan Stevenson*

Surrender. That most difficult challenge. It flies in the face of all we are taught to treasure and value in this world. It runs contrary to our deeply human need for control, or at the very least, for a sufficiently convincing perception of control. In approaching the sunrise this morning, a brief but clear message streamed across my headphones to surrender all that we are, *everything*, to the Lord. Every impulse I have wants to argue with this, to maintain an *Invictus* stance and cling fiercely to the notion that, "I am the master of my fate! I am the captain of my soul! (Invictus, William Ernest Henley)" Or perhaps, in a slightly less dramatic response, I may acquiesce to surrender *some* of myself, but certainly not all.

Yet the song calls us to surrender everything, and so does our Lord. James reminds us that "God opposes the proud, but gives grace to the humble." and he implores us to, "Submit yourselves then to God…come near to God and he will come near to you…Humble yourselves before the Lord and he will lift you up (James 4:6-10)." Even before Christ came to save us, Isaiah encouraged the Israelites to live in accordance with God's will, and assured them that if they did, their cries would be answered, guidance would be given, provisions would be made, brokenness would be mended, and they would find their joy in the Lord (Isaiah 58: 6-14). Surrender, and God will help you. It seems like a pretty great deal (one that we are in no way deserving of), so why is it so hard for us to fulfill our end of the bargain?

To start with, absolute surrender requires absolute trust. To willingly submit ourselves to another, we need to have indisputable faith that they are good, their intentions are pure, they are capable of doing what we rely upon them to do, and that they are as committed to us as they are to themselves. We have to know in our heart and feel in our bones that they hold our wellbeing and our future dearly and will act only in pursuit of our good. That kind of trust may seem like a lot, but consider the many small pockets of surrender we find and willingly engage in every single day. We trust our families, so we commend important decisions to their wisdom. We trust our teachers, and so we seek and employ their guidance. We even trust our airplane pilots and Uber drivers, and so we sit peacefully and await our safe arrival. In each of these situations, we willingly surrender a piece of control, and that piece is directly proportional to the depth of our trust and of our confidence that trust is well-placed. We will inevitably be more reserved, cautious, or skeptical when our trust feels shaky, but we will go all-in, vulnerably but faithfully, when our trust is firm and steadfast.

In these everyday acts of surrender, trust becomes not just a feeling, but a tangible deed. Our behaviors, actions, and reactions are changed and strengthened out of respect and reverence for the one we surrender to. We begin to act in ways that are pleasing to the other person or we honor rules and agreements for the relationship of trust we've formed. Why does it come so naturally, so easily, to surrender control in those pockets of our lives, but not with the one who has proven, time and time again throughout all history, that he is faithful? After all, we willingly – happily – change our behaviors out of love for our spouse and awareness of their hopes and needs. We release the reins of our children's education to their teachers out of faith in their credentials. Indeed, we automatically entrust our safety to the pilot we have never met operating the plane we did not build which stays aloft because of aerodynamics we probably do not understand. Yet, when God – the Father, the Creator, Lord Almighty, the Great I am – calls upon us to surrender, to honor his will and respect his preferences, to learn from his teachings and apply his instruction, to sit confidently and yield to the most capable captain of all, what do we do? We hesitate. Question. Argue. Challenge. We defend our way, ask him to go along with it, cling to our fears, and beg for control.

This struggle makes me think that perhaps surrender is not meant to be a single act of blind, all-encompassing submission, but rather a thousand acts every day, of intentional, informed, active trust. In his letter to the church in Rome, Paul writes, "Do not conform any longer to the pattern of this world, but be transformed by the renewing of your mind, so that you may discern what is the good, pleasing and perfect will of God (Romans 12:2)." Surrender is trust in action – it is not only proclaiming, but demonstrating, that we are not the masters of our fate nor the captains of our souls (with due respect to William Ernest Henley), but instead, that we believe and embrace the reality that a man's life is not his own, and it is not for man to direct his steps (Jeremiah 10:23). Because of the trust and unwavering faith we have in the power and goodness of our Lord, we can gladly, intentionally, fully, and actively surrender to him – one choice, one step, one action at a time.

### A Prayer

*Lord, thank you for being steadfast, even when I am not. Thank you for being faithful, even when I doubt. Thank you for being constant, even when I waiver. Help me today to submit to you once, with one small decision or one small action, help me to make the choice you would have me make. Then Lord, please help me to do it again, and then again, and then again. As I strengthen this habit, may I find overwhelming peace in my submission, and may I be found in awe of your work in my life. Amen.*

# Day Twenty-Two: Our Fathers' Wars

🎧 *Suggested Streaming: Meant to Live by Switchfoot*

Today is a day that cries out for inspiration and hope. As I look out all around me, I can feel a deep sense of urgency pulsing through my veins for a world that needs change-makers. A world that needs motivated, determined, galvanized people who love God, love each other, and serve the greater good. It is easy to become disheartened and frustrated in the repetition of our challenges – to become frustrated by a world that seems intent to repeat all the worst sins of its past. As I approached the sunrise this morning, my stirring heart was searching for encouragement to combat that "Groundhog Day" repetition, and the exhaustion of living in a world where we must fight all of yesterday's battles with none of tomorrow's strength. Absent that motivating fire, we are easily left asking, "why even bother, when nothing ever changes?", but instead, I cried out in agreement as Switchfoot sang into my headphones a demand for more than the conflicts and wars of generations past.

Amen! The song hung in the air, heavy in its truth and its gravity. Our fathers' wars – wars of race, status, security, sovereignty, liberty, justice, and opportunity. Generations follow generations, one after the other, but the wars stay the same. In Ecclesiastes, King Solomon penned the truth of this phenomenon nearly 3,000 years ago: "What has ben is what will be, and what has been done is what will be done; there is nothing new under the sun. (Ecclesiastes 1:9)". He goes on to say, "there is no remembrance of those who came before, and of those who will come after there will also be no remembrance by those who follow them (1:11)." To really drive the point home, in my CSB translation, these verses appear under a heading that reads "EVERYTHING IS FUTILE" (yes…in all caps). Admittedly, not a great start, but bear with me. The book of Ecclesiastes begins with what is essentially Solomon's description of life on earth without the peace and perspective of eternal salvation. In other words, if this is all there is, then yes, everything in the human existence is futile.

Fortunately, this is not all there is, and our eternal Father has a plan for our redemption. Solomon later notes that "for every activity there is a right time and procedure, even though a person's troubles are heavy on him

(Ecclesiastes 8:6)". When we live without God, and we frame our decisions and actions absent his guidance, our efforts will continue to produce all the same tragic results – as we continue to live with no remembrance of what came before, repeating all the same mistakes and transgressions of the generations before us. This tendency toward forgetfulness and rebellion is nothing new – "How often they rebelled against him in the wilderness and grieved him in the desert. They constantly tested God and provoked the Holy One of Israel…They treacherously turned away like their fathers. (Psalm 78: 40-41, 57).

If we honestly want more than the wars we've inherited, then we must abandon the ways our stubborn fathers lived. We must become what is new under the sun, and as King Solomon explains, this can only be done when we live in the reality and reverence of a God who is fully in control. When we live obediently, we live differently. We live as Paul implored the Romans when we told them, "Do not be conformed to this age, but be transformed by the renewing of your mind, so that you may discern what is the good, pleasing, and perfect will of God (Romans 12:2)."

Although the world will not be fully redeemed until Christ comes again, we have a chance (and an obligation) to do our part to break the chain. To usher some level of peace to the wars of our fathers and to become what is new under the sun, we must know, understand, and remember the sins of generations before us. To change the world, to begin breaking the cycles of our fathers, we must chose not to conform to the standards they set, instead fixing our eyes – and our hands, minds, hearts, and feet – on the Heavenly Father's example rather than a thousand generations of our earthly ones.

### *A Prayer*

*Lord, today I lift up a world that is broken, a world that needs you desperately, and that waits for your divine intervention. I ask you to break the chains of violence, injustice, war, and suffering that have been forged and lengthened by one generation after the other. I ask you to use me as a vessel to bring your peace to this land, and I pray that you will keep my eyes fixed on you and allow me to be transformed by your goodness rather than conformed to the sins of this age. Heal our world Lord and help us to love each other as you have loved us. Amen.*

# Day Twenty-Three: Forgive Yourself

🎧 *Suggested Streaming: Mercy is a Song by Matthew West*

Forgiveness is one of the hardest things to do – as a Christian and as a human. It goes against our natural inclinations and forces us to remove ourselves from dispensing judgement. To forgive is to acknowledge someone's wrongdoing, including the harm it caused, and to release that person from your condemnation. It means that you will not hold it over them, not hold it against them, not keep it in constant memory, and not drudge it up in some distant future. It means that while that person may deserve to answer for their actions, they will not answer to you. As Christians, we have the benefit of knowing the only true judge, and we know that God both forgives and holds accountable. Knowing these truths, we may find it easier (though still not easy) to be generous in our forgiveness of others, yet, we often don't extend that to the forgiveness of ourselves. This resonated with me today as I contemplated the lies we often tell ourselves about our guilt and our worthiness (or lack thereof) to be forgiven.

How can we learn to forgive those who hurt us, and even approach the throne of grace ourselves, to ask faithfully, knowingly, and expectantly for God's forgiveness, and yet we find it impossible to release ourselves from that iron grip of guilt? Perhaps, like so many things, the answer to this question is anchored in perspective. When we forgive others, our focus is typically on the act of forgiving. We offer forgiveness because the Lord has urged us to and because through his example, he has taught us how to. This is evident throughout the entirety of the New Testament, for example:

- Be kind and compassionate to one another, forgiving one another, just as God also forgave you in Christ (Ephesians 4:32).
- For if you forgive others their offenses, your heavenly Father will forgive you as well (Matthew 6:14).
- Bearing with one another and forgiving one another if anyone has a grievance against another. Just as the Lord has forgiven you, so you are also to forgive (Colossians 3:13).

- Do not judge, and you will not be judged. Do not condemn, and you will not be condemned. Forgive, and you will be forgiven (Luke 6:37).
- And whenever you stand praying, if you have anything against anyone, forgive him, so that your Father in heaven will also forgive you your wrongdoing (Mark 11:25).

We can follow this abundantly repeated guidance because our eyes are set on the actual act, virtue, process, and expectation of our charity through forgiveness.

In the same way, when we approach God to ask forgiveness for ourselves, our focus is often on the greatness, love, and mercy which form the very character and nature of God. We approach him knowing that he loves us, even though he knows every sin we've committed and every sinful inclination we've entertained. Indeed, he loves us so much that he gave his one and only son as a substitutionary sacrifice to ensure that our sin would not form a permanent barrier between us and him (John 3:16). The act wasn't predicated on our good and righteous behavior, which we know because God proves his love for us in that *while we were still sinners* Christ died for us (Romans 5:8). We are so assured of God's tremendous, unfailing, loving grace that when we ask his forgiveness, we do so with a focus on that foundational truth.

So, we can forgive others by focusing on God's teaching and examples of forgiveness, and we can ask forgiveness of the Father by focusing on his boundless love and mercy (which he offers freely). Why then, is it so hard to forgive ourselves? Why do we believe the lie that we don't deserve to be free?

Because our focus is on our sin. Our perspective is the gravity, depth, harm, repetition, and imprisonment of our failures, shortcomings, misdeeds, and mistakes. Instead of focusing on God's grace, we focus on how unworthy we are to receive it. The truth is that we do fall short, and we are unworthy – every one of us – but still, God extends to us the greatest gift we could ask for: cleanliness. He doesn't just hear our apology and ask that we do better, he *cleanses* us of our sins, which inspires and drives us to do better. When we focus on our sins, all we can do is try and move forward by simply managing our sins – and as every failed New Year's resolutions tells us, obsessively focusing on sin management very rarely generates long-lasting results.

God offers us more than a sin mitigation plan, he offers sin removal. Even before Christ came to earth, God extended an invitation to the Israelites: "Come, let us settle this. Though your sins are scarlet, they will be white as snow, though they are crimson red, they will be like wool (Isaiah 1:18)." Under the old covenant, this forgiveness was offered based on willing obedience to the law of God (Isaiah 1:19), but under the new covenant, we have become the righteousness of God – not we can access or petition, beg, and plead for his righteousness – we *are* the righteousness of God, because he who knew no sin became sin for us (2 Corinthians 5:21). We are the righteousness of God, so he cleanses us of all unrighteousness (1 John 1:9), he removes all condemnation because we are in Christ (Romans 8:1), he removes our transgressions as infinitely far as the east is from the west (Psalm

103:12), and he makes us new because our old selves – our sinful, hopeless selves – are dead (2 Corinthians 5:17). When we focus on this extraordinary truth, the truth that our sins are not only forgiven, but cleansed, removed, banished, and killed, the lie of guilt no longer stands up.

## A Prayer

*Heavenly Father, thank you for placing forgiveness at the heart of your nature. Thank you for teaching me and showing me how to forgive those who have harmed me. Thank you for extending grace I do not deserve by forgiving my sins and cleansing me of them entirely. Thank you, above all, for loving me so much that you came to earth and endured an unspeakable death in order to make that grace possible. Lord, I pray that you would help me today to release the guilt I have held on to. If you have cast my sins away, as far as the east is from the west, then please help me live into the beauty and fullness of the mercy you have given me. Amen.*

# Day Twenty-Four: Blessed

🎧 *Suggested Streaming: The Blessing by Elevation Worship, Kari Jobe, and Cody Carnes*

Today, looking out at a beautiful, peaceful, tranquil sunrise, the setting seems custom-made for the song playing as I approached it. As I looked out across the sky, I took a moment to close my eyes and just breathe as I listened to Elevation Worship, Kari Jobe, and Cody Carnes sing *The Blessing*. This beautiful song sets to music *The Priestly Blessing*, which the Lord gave to Moses to instruct Aaron and the priests on how to bless the Israelites. The comforting, inspiring words appear in Numbers 6:22-26:

> The Lord bless you and keep you
> Make His face shine upon you
> And be gracious to you
> The Lord turn His face toward you
> And give you peace

After giving him these words, God tells Moses, "In this way they will pronounce my name over the Israelites, and I will bless them (Numbers 6:27)." He specifically instructs Aaron (via Moses) to bless them like this in his name, which gives us an idea of how God wished to be perceived by his people. His people had witnessed the plagues in Egypt, so God could have easily instructed Aaron to portray him as fearsome and powerful, with a blessing that may be reminiscent of our parents' "do as I say, or else!" warnings. Or, having rescued and delivered the Israelites by parting the sea, the blessing may have been one of indebtedness, that we ought to obey because we owe God our compliance. God chose neither of these messages. Instead, he instructs Moses to give Aaron these words – a three-part blessing that assures God's people of his love for them.

The first part of the blessing is a message of protection. *May the Lord bless you and keep you* is a petition to God to provide for his people and to keep them safe – safe from danger, but also safe from evil, from sinful desires, from the temptation to turn away from the Lord. Why? Because the second part of the blessing – *May the Lord make his face shine upon you and be gracious to you* – is a prayer for relationship between God and his people. It is a request that the Lord would look upon his people, as a father looks upon his children, with a face that reflects his loving, joyful, hopeful nature. And what comes of that loving relationship? The third part of the blessing – favor and abounding peace: *May the Lord look with favor on you and give you peace.* God did not wish for his people to obey primarily out of fear (although he is due that respect) or out of obligation (although we owe a debt we can never repay ourselves). He wanted them to obey for the same reasons a child obeys a parent – because a parent protects them, loves them, favors them, and works to set them on a path toward a peaceful life. As Aaron pronounced the name of the Lord over the Israelites by blessing them in this way, he proclaimed the true nature of God.

While this beautiful, peaceful blessing came to some of the earliest of God's people, it is not hard to find parallels when we reflect on God's instructions to his New Covenant people. In Matthew 6:9-13, Jesus teaches us to pray:

Our Father, who art in Heaven
Hallowed by the name
Thy kingdom come
Thy will be done
On earth as it is in Heaven
Give us this day our daily bread
And forgive us our sins
As we forgive those who sin against us
And lead us not into temptation
But deliver us from the evil one

Here again we see a prayer for God's provision (to meet our daily needs) and protection (against temptation). Again we see a prayer for God's grace and fatherly example (in forgiveness), and again we see a call for his favor and everlasting peace (as his will is done and the kingdom of Heaven comes to earth). With almost 1,500 years separating the two texts, we can take comfort that the intention, nature, and desire of our God as loving, protective, nurturing, and peaceful is unchanging. There is an old Irish blessing that entreats, "May the blessings of each day be the blessings you need most". If the Lord blesses us, keeps us, makes his face shine upon us, is gracious, favors us, and gives us peace, then certainly those are exactly the blessings we need most!

### *A Prayer*

*Lord almighty, thank you for your boundless blessings. Thank you, that even though you are deserving of our fearful and indebted obedience, that what you truly desire is for us to follow you affectionately and to recognize our need for your provision and protection. Lord, would you help me to rely fully on you today, trusting that you will keep me in your protection, love me as your child, and bring me peace. Father, every blessing from you is the blessing I need most. Amen.*

# Day Twenty-Five: Letting Go

🎧 *Suggested Streaming: Burn the Ships by For King and Country*

It can be easy, tempting even, to live with one foot in the present and one in the past. When we keep one foot outside, it guarantees we have an escape if things should go badly. As I sat and watched the sun rising this morning, I did so while prayerfully facing an important crossroads in my life. As I prepared to take the next step on a new and unknown path, I did so desperately wanting to cling to pieces of the path I had traveled thus far. And yet, across my headphones came a timely song, urging (as the title suggests) me to burn the ships and not look back. At first, these instructions may feel harsh, but when we consider the power of reckless anticipation, anchored in God's unwavering faithfulness, they do not seem too severe at all. While memories can be a great source of comfort and nostalgia, if they hold a disproportionate share of our mind, those memories can quickly inhibit our potential either by offering an escape or by binding us too tightly to our past.

The order to "burn the ships" is an historic reference to Herran Cortes in the New World, circa 1519. Upon arriving on the shores of Veracruz, Cortes ordered his legion of 600 men to set their entire fleet ablaze. While the frugal conservationist in me is appalled by this, I understand and respect the symbolic and practical gesture. They arrived in the New World. It was a hard fought and hard-earned journey, and they had arrived. They had no idea what lay before them, but they knew the comfort of all they left behind. To retreat would be easy – to go back to the familiar, the known, the understood. How often do we pull back in retreat when faced with something scary or unexpected? How often do we stand still when we're afraid to take a new, unchartered path forward? How often does turning back feel easier, wiser even, than pressing on? In his order to burn the ships, Cortes categorically eliminated that choice. The message and the impact were clear: there is only one path forward, and there are no other options. With this strategy, Cortes was trying to send a similar message that God often conveys to us: there is enormous potential here and I have great plans for you, if only you would trust me enough to be all-in.

Burning the ships may definitely eliminate our options for retreat, but it's the last part of For King and Country's message that I find the most difficult – *don't look back*. This is not a call to forget the past and abandon all the memories, lessons and experiences we leave behind. Rather, it is an admonishment not to dwell in the past and not long for what we've left behind. If part of our hearts and minds are occupied with what we've lost, then we rid our present and future of the attention and mindshare they deserve.

This calls to mind the story of Abram's nephew Lot and his wife, as the couple fled the city of Sodom. The corrupt city was about to be demolished in a rain of brimstone and fire. Two angels of the Lord urged Lot to take his wife and daughters out of the city, but he hesitated. Out of compassion, the angels grabbed them by their hands and forced them to leave (Genesis 19:15-16). Once outside the city, Lot and his family were given clear instructions: "Run for your lives! Don't look back and don't stop…Hurry up! Run to it [Zoar, a nearby city], for I cannot do anything until you get there (Genesis 19:17-22)." As sulfuric rain assailed the entire plain, obliterating the cities of Sodom and Gomorah, Lot's wife looked back, and she was turned into a pillar of salt (Genesis 19:26).

It's only one sentence in the Old Testament, but it was so important that Jesus reminded his disciples of the fate of Lot's wife when he implored them to look toward the coming kingdom rather than clinging to the possessions and comforts of their past. He warns that on the day Heaven comes to earth, the man standing in the field must not turn back. "Remember Lot's wife!" he says before instructing them that whoever tries to make his life secure will lose it, and whoever loses his life will preserve it (Luke 17:32-33). The message is clear – in order to live fully as our whole and best selves, we must be willing to give our whole and best selves up. It may feel like a steep price to pay, but we must remember that when we entrust everything to the Lord, it's not a gamble. The angels who visited Lot and his family brought the assurance of safety and protection in exchange for their trust and obedience. Jesus offers something greater still for ours – eternal life and the glory of Heaven. When we understand and really internalize what lays ahead, we can gladly burn the ships and not look back.

### A Prayer

*God, thank you for giving me something greater than all I could leave behind. As you place new opportunities in my path, please give me the confidence to embrace them. As you place new challenges in my midst, please give me the strength to endure them. Help me to treasure the memories and experiences of my past, without longing for its comforts. Help me to burn the ships, knowing that I don't need a plan B when plan A leads to you. Grant me the conviction today Lord, to be all-in. Amen.*

# Day Twenty-Six: Refining Fire

🎧 *Suggested Streaming: Stars by Skillet*

One thing life has taught me is perspective. Pain, chaos, confusion, and fear are all relative, and we tend to measure and respond to them proportionally based on the worst outcome we've experienced or imagine. Of course, that means that when you have a fairly broad spectrum of experience in "worst case scenarios", it allows you to keep a more level head when things go wrong.

I always loved the Franklin D. Roosevelt quote, "still waters never made a skilled sailor." In sailing and in life, the hard truth is that we learn infinitely more in rough waters. Tactically, we learn to problem-solve, to assess the situation, to weigh the possible responses and outcomes, and to act (or react) accordingly. But a much, much more important lesson can also be learned when we are facing the crashing waves of life's stormiest waters – the lesson of relinquishing our perceived control in favor of a God who is faithful, powerful, and able to still the seas of our lives.

This morning as I walked toward the sunrise, the song "Stars" by Skillet played, and I listened to their powerful reminder that God is always able to calm the storm. The song calls to mind the story of Jesus in the boat with his disciples, in which Luke shares that Jesus fell asleep as they sailed into a massive storm. The disciples reacted just as most of us would…which is to say that they completely panicked. They saw the storm, they watched the waves in fear, and they perceived their Lord as "absent" in the midst of the chaos and danger. But Jesus was there – literally, in the boat with them – but he was also there in the sense that he was in control of all that felt uncontrollable. "He got up and rebuked the wind and the raging waters; the storm subsided, and all was calm (Luke 8:24)." With the threat now gone, Jesus asks his disciples a fair question: *Where is your faith?* And they stood in awe and amazement that even the most powerful forces of nature obeyed Jesus, the Son of God.

For me, this story stirs to fundamental questions in my heart. First, if Jesus was in control the whole time, why did the storm come at all? Why not just sail on through peaceful, calm waters? Second, why were Jesus' disciples, who had witnessed many miracles by this point, worried by the storm and surprised by his command over it? The first really is the age-old question, if God is all powerful, why do bad things happen? Well, to borrow from Mr. Roosevelt, hard times are necessary to improve – refine – our sailing skills that we may be prepared for all that God will call us to. The prophet Malachi compares the challenging, even painful, ways God prepares us to a refiner's fire (Malachi 3:2-3). I usually think of fire as a powerful, fierce, and destructive force – much the same way the disciples may have described the raging sea during the storm – but a *refiner's fire* is very different. It is careful, intentional, purposeful, and always under the control of the watchful refiner. It is still fire, it still burns, subdues, and inflicts pain, but for having endured the violent power of this fire, the gold and silver subjected to its flames emerge pure, beautiful, and ready to serve their intended purpose. They are made better for having experienced the flames, and they are made pure as the fire consumes and destroys the impurities they entered with.

We often fear that the fires in our lives will incinerate us, but God – the Refiner – will always faithfully pull us from the flames; always in his perfect timing, not leaving us to suffer a moment longer than we must, but also not removing the burden of the fire before its purpose is served entirely. The fires of loss, grief, fear, anger, confusion, and regret shape and refine us in ways that nothing else possibly could. Perhaps most profoundly, they instill confidence in our hearts that the Refiner is always in control and always tending the flames which purify our hearts. With this truth in the front of our minds, instead of reacting as the disciples did in the crashing storm, we can turn to the one who is in control and trust him to both use our pain to teach and prepare us, and also to protect us from the fire's destructive force.

### *A Prayer*

*Heavenly Father, thank you for carefully navigating me through both the smooth waters and turbulent storms of my life. I know that hard times, while painful and frustrating, shape me and prepare me for the good and important works you have planned. Lord, please give me strength to endure the challenges I face, wisdom to learn from these experiences, and humility to submit to your refining, purifying, forming, and shaping fire. Amen.*

# Day Twenty-Seven: Dry Bones

🎧 *Suggested Streaming: Come Alive (Dry Bones) by Lauren Daigle*

It struck me this morning that the garden I write from feels very much like my own little personal piece of Eden. I come here, and I find peace. Rabbits, squirrels, and the occasional fox come and go, seemingly unaware – or at least unconcerned – of my presence. I commune with God here, and I can talk with him as though he is sitting on the bench next to me. Nothing is off limits because he knows every hair on my head, every thought on my mind, and every concern on my heart. For these precious twenty or thirty minutes each day, I have the privilege of catching a small glimpse of creation as the Creator himself intended it to be.

As captivating as these moments are, I have to remind myself that they are incomplete, imperfect, and fleeting – because this isn't Eden, it is a breathtaking sunrise in a beautiful park, but it exists (as do we) in a broken world. When this moment passes, I know the real world will be waiting, along with obligations I can't satisfy, expectations I fall short of, and needs I don't meet. With all our personal battles, coupled with newsfeeds and airwaves overtaken by anger, fear, and injustice, it's easy to wonder if things are just too far gone to ever be redeemed. Even on a less global scale, how often do we ask the same question about ourselves? Am I beyond saving?

As I indulge myself with a few more minutes in this thin shade of Eden, I'm listening to Lauren Daigle beckoning to dry bones, "Come alive!". The *Vision of the Valley* is one of the most compelling stories you could ask for. In it, we find God leading the prophet Ezekiel through a vast valley filled with bones – bones so old, so profoundly lifeless, that they were completely dry. I imagine them as being so brittle that they would be crushed into dust if Ezekiel allowed an errant foot to brush upon one. To borrow from *A Christmas Carol*, these bones were as decidedly dead as Jacob Marley – which is to say, as dead as a doornail. And to again quote the prodigious Charles Dickens, "this must be distinctly understood, or nothing wonderful can come of the story."

In the valley, God asks Ezekiel a seemingly simple question: Can these bones live? (Ezekiel 37:3). Ezekiel was a man of tremendous faith who lived in close communion with the Lord; yet, he was still human, and so I have to believe his first thought looking across that chasm of dead-as-a-doornail bones was "NOPE! They are dead…very, very dead. They are beyond saving." But instead of focusing on the lifelessness of the dry bones or the magnitude of the graven valley, Ezekiel focuses instead on the might, power, and faithfulness of God. Rather than reply as his instincts or the evidence might suggest, he replies boldly, "Lord God, only you know (Ezekiel 37:3)". It's five simple words, but contained within them is an affirmation of faith in the almighty, an acquiescence of human logic, and a profession of hope in the impossible. Anchored in his steadfast faith, Ezekiel does as God commands and speaks to the bones until, through the power of God, they reassemble themselves, are bound with tendons and flesh, and life is breathed into them. Ezekiel witnessed the expanse of dry bones come to life as an army of Israel.

Importantly, this vision was used by God as a metaphor for Israel. God's people had been scattered, oppressed by the Babylonian Empire, and were seemingly without any hope for reunification or restoration. The Israelites were, for all intents and purposes, a valley of dry bones. Doesn't it feel that way for us too? In the midst of arguments and power struggles, ideological stalemate, corruption and injustice, not to mention the occasional exhaustion of simply living, doesn't it often feel that perhaps we are just too far gone to be restored and reunified? Or as we ourselves fall into the same patterns of selfishness, temptation, and sin, does it ever feel like we have gone too far to be redeemed?

The story of the dry bones teaches us three monumentally important truths. First, there is immeasurable peace and power in seeing problems not by the depth of the challenge, but by the abundance of God's authority. When we fully internalize this reality, nothing – not even Jacob Marley-level, dead-as-a-doornail death – can overwhelm us. Secondly, God will always do as he promises, and we neither can nor need to understand how. God raised an army from the valley of dry bones, just as he did indeed reunite his people Israel, and just as he did send the promised Messiah to redeem us all, and just as he has fulfilled every word of every promise he has ever made. We can steadfastly, unwaveringly, undoubtedly rely on God's faithfulness. Finally, that these first two truths apply to everything – every person, every nation, every situation, no matter how big, how small, nor how seemingly dry the bones are, God's power is limitless and his reliability uncontested.

### *A Prayer*

*Father God, thank you for breathing life into our dry bones. Thank you for redeeming us, even when we feel like a lost cause. Lord, I have confidence in your faithfulness, and I know that you will never abandon me. I pray that you would continue moving in the midst of conflict in our world and conflict in my heart. I pray that you would bring arguing nations and arguing people to reconciliation, bring polarizing views to common ground, bring insurmountable challenges to unprecedented victories, and bring my own heart closer to you. Help me to remember that nothing is ever too far gone for you to redeem it fully, and beyond my wildest imagination. Amen.*

# Day Twenty-Eight: Day by Day
🎧 *Suggested Streaming: Great is Thy Faithfulness (hymn)*

I am not a fan of platitudes. Those well-intentioned phrases we offer one another when we can't find the words we really want to say, or when words simply fall short. We tell each other "this too shall pass" or "look on the bright side" instead of acknowledging that this valley is dark, this time is painful, and while we may know and believe that there is purpose in it, that doesn't ease our present suffering. I'll also admit that I am a serial offender when it comes to offering up the glass-half-full, sunshine-all-the-time perspective. Even so, the one phrase that even I try carefully to avoid is this: "It is what it is." Have five words ever been more meaningless? I suppose we can't argue its accuracy, but I am bothered by the hopelessness the sentiment conjures. The implication seems to be "it is what it is…and nothing can be done about it." If nothing can be done, then our only options are to wallow in incurable sadness or fight futilely to no real end. But God calls us to do more. Our confidence in the absolute power and loving nature of God calls us to believe rather than to wallow or toil. To the world "it is what it is"…but to God, it is anything but. It is what he wills – or has willed – it to be.

The truth is, we need more than platitudes in the face of our challenges. We need real support, real guidance, and real direction. With that in mind, I listened intently as the words of yet another favorite hymn streamed through my headphones: "Great is thy faithfulness! Morning by morning new mercies I see. All I have needed thy hand hath provided. Great is thy faithfulness, Lord unto me (Great is Thy Faithfulness, Thomas Chisholm)." These lyrics, which borrow from Lamentations 3:23, reflect the joy and promise we feel as we sing them in worship on a Sunday morning. A closer look, however, at the preceding verses in Lamentations reveals the deep sadness the author felt, and that we tend to feel, in life's messiest moments.

Before proclaiming God's faithfulness, the author of Lamentations professes that he continually remembers his afflictions, has forgotten his prosperities, and feels that his future is lost. In this sad state, he admits that he has become depressed (Lamentations 3:17-20). Sure, he's much more eloquent in his delivery, but we can almost hear the 580 BC-era writer crying out in grief, "Alas! It is what it is." Fortunately, he doesn't stop there, and nor should we. He turns his thoughts to the Lord's faithful love, and it gives him hope. He proclaims that the Lord's mercies are unending, and as the song echoes, they are new every morning, for great is the Lord's faithfulness! (Lamentations 3:21-23). It's important to note that the author's grief was not insubstantial, nor was his advice the stuff of platitudes. Despite the depth of his mourning, he writes that the path to peace is to turn our thoughts away from our grief, and to instead recall God's abundant grace.

Similar advice is given centuries later in Paul's letter to the church in Philippi, where he urges followers to find God's peace through prayer, petition, and gratitude, and to focus their minds by dwelling on things that are honorable, just, pure, lovely, commendable, excellent, and praiseworthy (Philippians 4:6-8). On first blush, both the testimony in Lamentations and the guidance in Philippians may read as platitudes and may feel just as shallow (as may the hymn, *Great is Thy Faithfulness*), but they are real, practical, hands-on solutions for finding God's transcendent peace. When we are hurting, lost, frustrated, or feeling hopeless, we are told peace is found by doing these things:

1. Recall to memory how the Lord has protected you in the past (Lamentations 3:22).
2. Acknowledge in prayer what it is you are troubled by – give it a name – then ask for God's intervention and thank him for his love and mercy (Philippians 4:6).
3. Filter out the lies (including the ones you are telling yourself) and focus on what is true in your situation (Philippians 4:8a).
4. Ask yourself what a fair and just outcome would be (Philippians 4:8b). It's easy to focus only on the outcome we hope for or would devise for ourselves, but how might that outcome harm someone else? Is there another way you haven't yet considered, or maybe even imagined?
5. Consider everything in your circumstances that is pure, lovely, and praiseworthy (Philippians 4:8c). Spend time in reflection and in deep, deep gratitude for those things. Hold each in your mind and heart and allow them to overpower your grief. If only for a moment, allow God's peace to overwhelm you.
6. Repeat. God's mercies are new every morning not because they expire or may be exhausted, but because we need them each and every day.

### A Prayer

*Heavenly Father, thank you for your faithfulness, which is greater than I can fathom, and more than I could ever deserve. And thank you for your Word, which offers so much more than the clichés and platitudes we often offer each other. Help me to remember that your mercies are new each morning, and so is my need for your grace. Please also help me to govern my own thoughts, and to focus on your power above the circumstances I face, your truth above the lies I hear, and your joy above the pain I feel. Help me to remember all the times you have carried me through, and to have faith that you will again today. Amen.*

# Day Twenty-Nine: Unlikely Victories

🎧 *Suggested Streaming: The Father's House by Cory Asbury*

Everybody loves an underdog. We can't help it – there's just something about that unexpected victory for the noble, but disadvantaged, contender. We identify with the underdog because we want to believe, need to believe, that when the deck is stacked against us, we can still prevail.

The Bible is brimming with the accounts and testimonies of the most unlikely heroes, all of whom triumphed through God's grace alone. You may immediately call to mind the likes of David, the shepherd son of a farmer who defeated Goliath the giant. Or perhaps you think of Daniel, who emerged unscathed after being bound for an entire night in the lion's den. The song playing this morning brought to mind another unlikely hero, and a victory even less likely. The Battle of Jericho, and the story of Joshua, is an inspiring, but baffling, story of triumph through faith alone. In it, we find an unqualified leader, aided by an unexpected ally, leading an unprepared army with an impossible battle strategy. A recipe for disaster by any measure, but God doesn't conform to our standards for success.

Let's start with our humble leader, Joshua. To say Joshua came from humble beginnings is an understatement. A slave in Egypt, born to a long line of slaves, Joshua witnessed (and endured) the plagues of Egypt (Exodus 7-11) and survived on God's provisions of manna while wandering the desert through 40 years of exile (Exodus 16). Joshua had neither rank nor entitlement, no special training, and no advanced learning, but he possessed something much more valuable: unshakable faith in God's provision. I have always loved the saying "God doesn't call the qualified, he qualifies the called" – and Joshua is a shining example of the truth of that sentiment. On the one hand, we can say Joshua endured tremendous suffering in Egypt and in the desert, but on the other hand, we can plainly see how God was using those experiences to prepare him for the pivotal role he would play. As a slave, Joshua learned the deference and humility he would need to submit to Moses as God's chosen leader. When fleeing Egypt, he learned to trust God to create impossible pathways to victory – pathways that could even cross straight through the raging sea. While in exile, Joshua learned to rely on God to meet his needs, not his own planning, skill, or ability.

It was because of these hard lessons that Joshua was prepared to carry out God's instruction at Jericho. But before Joshua led the Israelites into the Promised Land, God provided him an unexpected helper and protector. Rahab, known better as "Rahab the prostitute" acted in tremendous faith, and against her own countrymen, by courageously hiding Joshua's spies whom he sent to scout Jericho. In doing so, she affirmed her own faith by telling them she knew the Lord had given this land to the Jews, and that she greatly feared the power of God, having heard of his great and miraculous deeds. Out of that fear, awe, and reverence, Rahab protected the spies and asked only for their protection in return – when the Lord fulfilled his promise and gave them the land, that she and her family would be spared. Because of Rahab's brave, defiant, and faithful intervention, the spies returned safely to Joshua and reported all they had learned (including the fear and panic harbored by the city's inhabitants) (Joshua 2-3). Despite her humble status and immoral profession, God used Rahab in a powerful way to change the course of Israel's history.

So we have our chosen, but unqualified leader, Joshua, and his delivered, but unexpected ally, Rahab – now to the battle. Victory is assured, God has already told his people that the land is theirs, so all that remains is the fight. Have you ever known exactly what God was calling you to do, but it seemed too outlandish to work? Well, here's the game plan… first, sound the trumpets and march silently around the city one time. Then return to camp and do nothing. Tomorrow, do it again. And the next day. And the next, and the next, and the next. Finally, on the seventh day, march around the city seven times, blow the trumpets, and shout as loudly as you can. Trust me. This will work.

I can just imagine Joshua's reaction…"umm…what??!"

But Joshua had been chosen uniquely by God and carefully groomed for this moment. Anyone else may have doubted, may have rushed in with their own brilliant battle strategy, or at least a solid plan B in their back pocket. But not Joshua. Joshua knew that a promise from God wasn't just "good as done" – it was already done. Joshua was all-in. When he told the Israelites the battle plan, he didn't preface it with "I know this sounds absurd" or hedge it with "if this doesn't work…". He planned to win because he planned unquestioningly for God to fulfill his promise. He obeyed and executed God's battle plan, and the walls of Jericho – the heavily fortified, well-guarded walls of Jericho – collapsed at his feet.

When we face battles of our own, how often do we approach them with our own plans first? Conventional wisdom tells us how we ought to fight, and we pray that God will make our plans successful. Instead, we should thank God for the victory he has already secured, recognize how he has prepared us for the fight ahead, pray for unexpected helpers and supporters along the way, and then follow his instructions faithfully – never doubting the victory, no matter how unlikely.

### A Prayer

*Father, I am so grateful for the awesome victories you have secured – throughout the history of the world, and in my own life. Please help me to remember that no matter how unlikely the odds, there is nothing you can't do, and nothing you won't do, to protect me. Father, I may not understand now, but I have faith that you are preparing me, teaching me, grooming me. Thank you for giving me a part to play in this fight, thank you for the people you have sent to help – even the ones I never expected – and help me Lord, to see your strategy through to the very end. Amen.*

# Day Thirty: Curiosity and Vulnerability

🎧 *Suggested Streaming: O Come to the Alter by Elevation Worship*

Do you know how many times a day I apologize for my curiosity? I'm sorry, I know I'm asking a lot of questions. I realize it's not my place to ask, I'm sorry for overstepping. I hope you don't mind me asking, I really don't mean to pry. The truth is, I can't help myself. I have an insatiable desire to understand everything that is within my human grasp to. With the normal cacophony of 10,000 questions running through my mind, I approached the sunrise today as Elevation Worship broke through, singing beautiful and timely questions of their own – specifically, do you need to go to the well? Is it time for a drink of living water?

A drink from the well – what a perfectly timed reference to another unapologetically curious truth-seeker, the woman at the well. Jesus' conversation with the Samaritan woman is longer than any interaction recorded in the Gospel of John between Jesus and any other person (John 4:1-26), which is fortunate because it was a conversation that we can all probably relate to. Indeed, one of the most important parts of their conversation is that it happened at all. In those times, Jews did not associate with Samaritans (John 4:9), and this was not only a Samaritan, but a *woman*. On top of that, this was a woman who either by social pressure or of her own accord, was an outsider, opting to fill her water jug alone in the afternoon rather than socializing at the well in the morning with other Samaritans. Despite being a Samaritan, a woman, and an outsider to boot, Jesus validates the woman's dignity and her inherent worth and value by simply speaking to her. He gave her access to the almighty, and invited her freely, eagerly, into a dialog.

The woman did as I no doubt would have (and frequently do) – she seized the opportunity to pepper him with questions. Why are you speaking to me? Don't you know I'm a Samaritan? What is this water of life? How will you get it from such a deep well? Don't you have a bucket? Are you greater than Jacob, who gave us this well? Did you know he drank from it, as did his sons and livestock? Of course, all these questions would have been more than satisfied had she only asked the one that really mattered: Who are you? She did not make that pivotal inquiry, but as he often does, Jesus answered the one question on her heart, rather than the dozens of questions on her lips. He would tell the woman who he was – who he really was – but first, before revealing the awesome, wonderful truth of his identity, Jesus pressed the curious Samaritan to get personal.

To truly know God, we must be willing to give up all pretenses and embrace the vulnerable position of engaging with someone who truly knows us – intimately, with no veneer, no window dressing, no guard. To break through those walls, Jesus implores the woman to go get her husband – a discussion she tries to deflect by simply saying that she does not have one (John 4:17). To be fair, her response is not a lie, and yet Jesus doesn't want to know us on the surface level of our partial truths. Jesus presses her: okay, yes, that's technically true…but I know that you have had five husbands and the man you have now is not your husband (John 4:18). Our deep, unvarnished truths are the ones we tend to conceal and cling to. Jesus sees those truths and he assures us that he knows our heart. He knows our story. He knows all the hope and all the baggage we are bringing to the conversation. He invites us to start there – unveiled.

Now, with all pretense abandoned, the woman acknowledges that Jesus is clearly a prophet and finally she goes for the questions that really matter – questions that will advance her search for true, meaningful worship. She probes Jesus: Our ancestors worshiped at the mountain in Samaria, but the Jews said we are to worship in Jerusalem. Which is right? How am I to worship so that I may draw nearer to God? This opens the door for Jesus to share that soon God would be worshipped fully in spirit and in truth by his people everywhere. With this good news, he goes on to reveal who he really is, that he is the Messiah, and that the prophecies which foretold his coming are fulfilled.

Well…that changes things. ***That. Changes. Everything.***

The woman leaves behind her water jug and goes immediately into town to tell all who would listen about this man. Despite her earlier desire to avoid the crowds, she sought them out to proclaim Christ's presence to her fellow townspeople; and despite the fact that she didn't have all the details her curious mind may have liked, she shared boldly the two truths that she did know: that this man knew her story, and that he may be the Messiah. Although an outsider, we know that the Samaritan woman held at least enough standing and credibility for her countrymen to take her seriously. Upon hearing her testimony, they invited Jesus to stay in Samaria. After just two days, we are told that many more believed in Jesus and proclaimed that he truly was the Savior of the World (John 4:39-42).

In many ways, this powerful story epitomizes my own journey and my reasons for writing this set of devotionals. It may also speak to some of your reasons for reading it. I began this journey feeling curious and confused, seeking answers to a million questions that I couldn't fully form. As we take time each day to meet with Jesus, he patiently hears our questions, but first he calls us to acknowledge all that we try to hide beneath the surface. Jesus wants our questions – those we can articulate and those we can't – but he also demands that we bring our whole selves to the conversation – every joyful, broken, complicated, messy, hopeful, painful, shameful, doubting, scared, optimistic, and anxious piece. And as we approach him each day as ourselves – our whole, imperfect, unveiled selves – he reminds us that he is God, that he knows our story, that he loves us completely, and he advocates for us fully. I am unspeakably grateful for these truths, still curious about the meaning of it all, still learning to be vulnerable, and, like the Samaritan woman, thrilled and eager to share this life-changing news with you, through these humble pages.

## *A Prayer*

*Thank you, Jesus, for engaging with me openly, honestly, and eagerly. Thank you for satisfying my curiosity to know you, and yet fueling it with a need and a desire to continue learning more. Lord, I pray that you would commune with me as you did with the Samaritan at the well. In your abundance, grant me humility to accept that my wisdom and understanding have limitations; confidence to bring my questions to you boldly; faith to know that you are God; and courage to share that truth with all who are willing to listen. I pray that you would never fully satisfy my curiosity, that I may always seek to know you more and more. Amen.*

# *About the Author*

Fueled by an insatiable sense of curiosity and an eager desire to know and understand the truth, Brittany Wilhelm has never met a question that didn't lead her to ask at least twelve more. Anchored by her reliance and faith in Jesus Christ, it was that desire for deeper understanding that inspired her debut book, Chasing the Son. Brittany is a native Coloradan, a graduate of the University of Denver, and lover of the written word. She, along with her husband Chris and their son Alex, now lives in Massachusetts where she serves on the staff of Harvard University.

Learn more about Brittany and discover more of her writing at www.HumilityHeartandHustle.com.

*And what does the Lord require of you? To act justly, to love mercy, and to walk humbly with your God. (Micah 6:8)*